Computing Made Simple

Access 2000
STEPHEN
0750641827   1999

Access 2000 Business Edition
STEPHEN
075064611X   1999

Access 97 for Windows
STEPHEN
0750638001   1997

CompuServe 2000   NEW!
BRINDLEY
0750645245   2000

Designing Internet Home Pages
2nd edition
HOBBS
0750644761   1999

ECDL/ICDL Version 3.0   NEW!
CD
0750651873   2000

Excel 2000
MORRIS
0750641800   2000

Excel 2000 Business Edition
MORRIS
0750646098   2000

Excel 97 for Windows
MORRIS
0750638028   1997

Excel for Windows 95 (V. 7)
MORRIS
0750628162   1996

Explorer 5
MCBRIDE, P K
0750646276   1999

Frontpage 2000
MCBRIDE, Nat
0750645989   1999

FrontPage 97
MCBRIDE, Nat
0750639415   1998

iMac and iBook   NEW!
BRINDLEY
075064608X   2000

Internet In Colour
2nd edition
MCBRIDE, P K
0750645768   1999

Internet for Windows 98
MCBRIDE, P K
0750645636   1999

MS DOS
SINCLAIR
0750620692   1994

Office 2000
MCBRIDE, P K
0750641797   1999

Office 97
MCBRIDE, P K
0750637986   1997

Outlook 2000   NEW!
MCBRIDE, P K
0750644141   2000

Photoshop
WYNNE-POWELL
075064334X   1999

Pocket PC   NEW!
PEACOCK
0750649003   2000

Powerpoint 2000
STEPHEN
0750641770   1999

Powerpoint 97 for Windows
STEPHEN
0750637994   1997

Publisher 2000
STEPHEN
0750645970   1999

Publisher 97
STEPHEN
0750639431   1998

Sage Accounts
McBRIDE
0750644133   1999

Searching the Internet
MCBRIDE, P K
0750637943   1998

Windows 98
MCBRIDE, P K
0750640391   1998

Windows 95
MCBRIDE, P K
0750623063   1995

Windows CE
PEACOCK
0750643358   1999

Windows ME   NEW!
MCBRIDE, P K
0750652373   2000

Windows NT
HOBBS
0750635118   1997

Word 2000
BRINDLEY
0750641819   1999

Word 2000 Business Edition
BRINDLEY
0750646101   2000

Word 97 for Windows
BRINDLEY
075063801X   1997

Word 7 for Windows 95
BRINDLEY
0750628154   1996

Works 2000
MCBRIDE, P K
0750649852   2000

UPCOMING in 2001

Basic Computer Skills
SHERMAN
075064897X

ECDL/ICDL 3.0
Office 2000 Edition
BCD
0750653388

Microsoft Project 2000
MURPHY
0750651903

ALL YOU NEED TO GET STARTED!

MADE SIMPLE BOOKS

Programming
Made Simple

C Programming
SEXTON
0750632445   1997

C++ Programming
SEXTON
0750632437   1997

COBOL
SEXTON
0750638346   1998

Delphi Version 5   NEW!
MORRIS
0750651881   2000

Delphi
MORRIS
0750632461   1997

HTML 4.0
MCBRIDE
0750641789   1999

Java
MCBRIDE, P K
0750632410   1997

Javascript
MCBRIDE, P K
0750637978   1997

Pascal
MCBRIDE, P K
0750632429   1997

Visual Basic
MORRIS
0750632453   1997

Visual C++
MORRIS
0750635703   1998

UPCOMING in 2001

Visual Basic Version 6
MORRIS
075065189X

ALL
YOU NEED
TO GET
STARTED!

MADE SIMPLE
BOOKS

Office XP
Made Simple

P.K. McBride

MADE SIMPLE
BOOKS

OXFORD AUCKLAND BOSTON JOHANNESBURG MELBOURNE NEW DELHI

Made Simple
An imprint of Butterworth-Heinemann
Linacre House, Jordan Hill, Oxford OX2 8DP
225 Wildwood Avenue, Woburn MA 01801-2041
A division of Reed Educational and Professional Publishing Ltd

Ɛ A member of the Reed Elsevier plc group

First published 2002
© P.K. McBride 2002

TRADEMARKS/REGISTERED TRADEMARKS
Computer hardware and software brand names mentioned in this book are protected
by their respective trademarks and are acknowledged.

British Library Cataloguing in Publication Data
A catalogue record for this book is available from the British Library.

ISBN 0 7506 5562 3

⚜ Typeset by Elle and P.K. McBride, Southampton
Icons designed by Sarah Ward © 1994
Printed and bound in Great Britain

Contents

Preface

Microsoft Office is the world's leading business application software suite. Office XP, the latest version, offers even better integration with the Web and more efficient team-working. The Office XP suite comes in several editions. All contain:

- **Word** – a word processor that is easy to use, yet has most of the features of a desktop publishing (DTP) package;
- **Excel** – a spreadsheet that is powerful enough to handle the accounts of a multi-million pound company, yet simple enough for a child to use for a school project;
- **PowerPoint** – presentation software, for producing slideshows and accompanying handouts and notes;
- **Outlook** is a comprehensive organiser, serving as a diary, job planner, address book, mail centre and more.

Depending upon the edition, you may also have:

- **Access** – a richly featured and powerful database system;
- **FrontPage** – for creating professional Web pages and managing Web sites;
- **Publisher** – desktop publishing software;
- **Small Business Customer Manager** and **Small Business Financial Manager**, integrated tools for businesses.

Office XP also has a large set of minor applications that are mainly run from within a major program. These include:

- software to add clip art, graphs, equations, charts, and decorative text to Word or Powerpoint documents;
- converters to read files from other word-processors, spreadsheets and databases into Office applications, and to save files in formats suitable for other systems;
- graphics filters to handle many different formats;
- DataMap to display regional data from Excel and Access on maps.

Take note

This book concentrates on the common features and core applications.

Office applications are huge, but they don't have to swamp your hard disk. Many of the optional features and less commonly-used components can be run from the CDs, or installed from the CDs if and when they are needed. This is worth considering if you are short of hard disk space, but note that it significantly slows down operations.

This book is really intended for people who are new to the Office applications. It concentrates on the features that are common to all and the core skills within each application, and should give you the foundations on which to develop your own understanding and expertise. If you have already used an earlier version of Office, you will have no difficulty in transferring your skills across to XP – there is very little new to learn here.

Office XP Made Simple assumes that you have a working knowledge of Windows. You should know how to use a mouse, handle windows, menus, toolbars and dialog boxes, and select text and objects on screen. If you need more guidance on any of this, there are *Made Simples* on Windows 98, Me, NT and XP.

Take note

To run Office XP efficiently, you need at least a 400Mhz Pentium, with 64 Mb of RAM (Windows 98/Me/NT) or 128Mb of RAM (Windows 2000), 250 Mb hard disk space and a VGA 800 x 640 monitor.

1 Office management

Starting work

There are several ways to start Office applications.

The Start menu

You can start any application from the Start menu – they will all have been addded to it at installation. In fact, they will all have been thrown into the Programs group and this may make the menu over-complicated. This is not a problem with the smart menus of Windows Me/XP. but on older systems you might want to reorganise the Start menu.

Tip

Set up desktop shortcuts to those applications that you use most often.

New and Open Documents can be moved off the main menu if you prefer

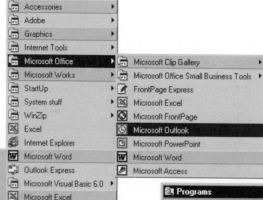

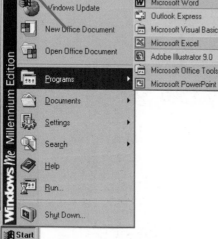

Use Start > Settings > Taskbar & Start menu then click the Advanced option. This opens the Start menu in Explorer. Create a new folder if you want a new submenu. Drag shortcuts to reorganise the menu

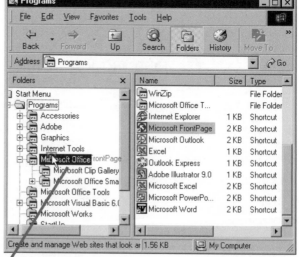

Starting from documents

The **New** and **Open Office Document** shortcuts – initially on the main menu – offer quick ways to start work on a file. This approach is good where you are mainly working on one document, rather than on a number within one application.

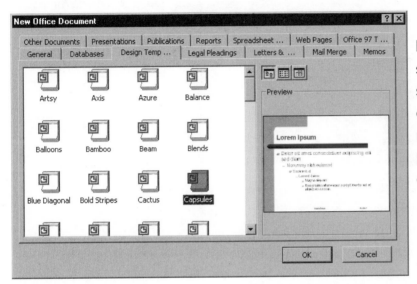

For a new document, switch to the tab, then select a template, wizard or blank document of the right type. The preview pane will give you an idea of the style and layout.

Files can be listed in several ways. Click the Views button to cycle through the views, or click the down arrrow and select one from the list

On the Open Document panel, you can find your recently used Office files in the History view. Just click on the name to open the document in its application.

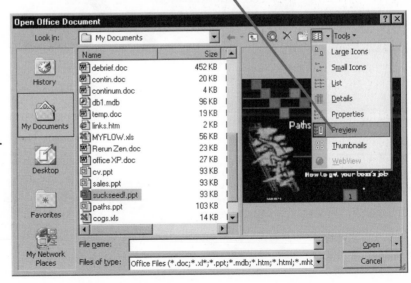

The Office Shortcut bar

The Office Shortcut bar comes equipped with buttons for opening or creating new Office files, adding tasks, contacts or appointments. You can also add shortcuts to Office (and other) applications.

When you first open the bar, you will be asked if you want it to open automatically on startup. Click 'Yes' if you do.

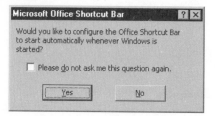

The shape and position the bar can be changed to suit your way of working. The bar can be a strip along any edge of the screen, or a floating strip or block. On an edge, it can be set to Auto Hide so that it disappears after use, and reappears when you point into that edge.

Basic steps

❏ Moving the Toolbar

1 Point to an empty part of the bar.

2 Drag to wherever you want it on the screen – to place it at an edge, push it slightly over.

❏ Adjusting the shape

3 Point to a side, to get the double-arrow cursor.

4 Drag to resize.

❏ Setting Auto Hide

5 Click the square at the top left of the Toolbar to open the menu.

6 Click to turn Auto Hide on ✓ or off.

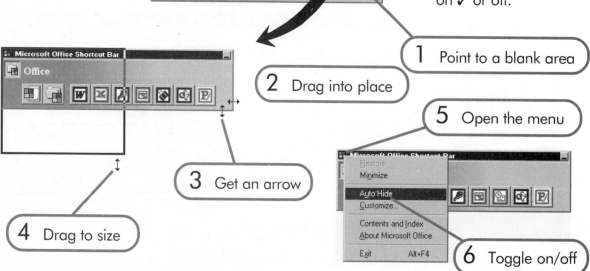

1 Point to a blank area

2 Drag into place

5 Open the menu

3 Get an arrow

4 Drag to size

6 Toggle on/off

Basic steps

1 Right-click on the toolbar to open the short menu.

2 Select Customize.

3 Open the Buttons panel.

4 Pick a Toolbar.

5 Click the □ box to add or remove a button.

6 Click ☐ OK ☐.

Customising the Shortcut bar

The most useful changes you can make to the Shortcut toolbar are to add to it buttons for the applications that you use – and remove unused ones. But you can also tailor its appearance, and you should check the **Settings** tab as this tells Office where to look for templates (see page 36).

● As well as adding shortcuts from the Office set, you can also add a link to any other program on your system, or to a folder.

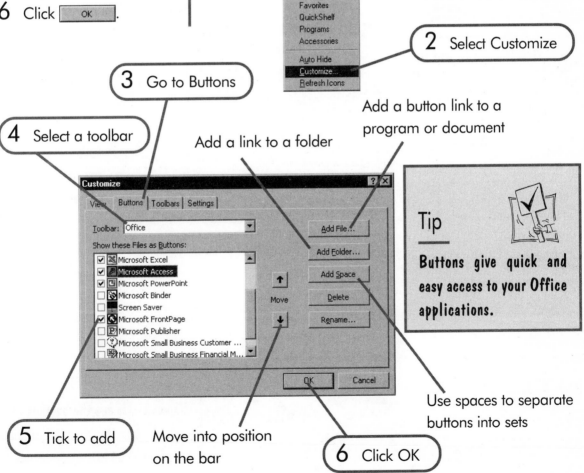

1 Open the short menu

2 Select Customize

3 Go to Buttons

4 Select a toolbar

Add a link to a folder

Add a button link to a program or document

Tip

Buttons give quick and easy access to your Office applications.

5 Tick to add

Move into position on the bar

6 Click OK

Use spaces to separate buttons into sets

Multiple bars

An Office toolbar represents a folder. Its shortcuts, programs and subfolders become items on the bar.

If you like the toolbar approach, you can create your own folder of shortcuts to favourite programs and make that into a toolbar.

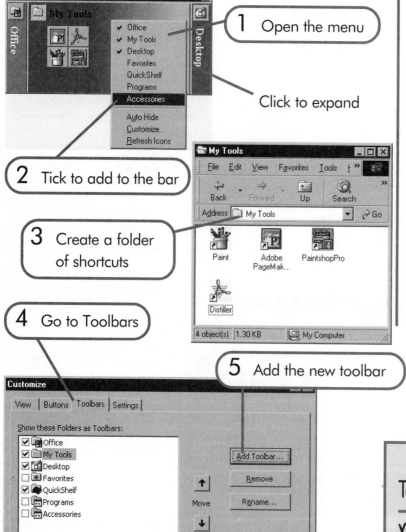

1 Open the menu

Click to expand

2 Tick to add to the bar

3 Create a folder of shortcuts

4 Go to Toolbars

5 Add the new toolbar

❑ Adding toolbars

1 Right-click in a clear part of the Toolbar, to get the short menu.

2 Click on the name to add a toolbar.

❑ Creating toolbars

3 In Explorer, create a new folder and store in it shortcuts to your selected programs.

4 Open the Customize panel from the short menu and select Toolbars.

5 Click Add Toolbar and browse for the new shortcut folder.

Take note

You can only see the buttons of one toolbar at a time. Click on a compressed bar to open it up.

Basic steps

1 Right-click on the toolbar to open the short menu.

2 Select Customize.

3 Open the View panel.

4 In the Colors pane, select the Toolbar then pick the Color and Fill style.

5 Try out any Options that seem worthwhile – you can always reset them again.

6 Click OK .

Changing views

You can change the colour, button size and other aspects of the Toolbar displays, using the View panel.

The Options apply to all toolbars, though the Colour choices only apply to the selected toolbar.

3 Open the View panel

These make Toolbars easier to use

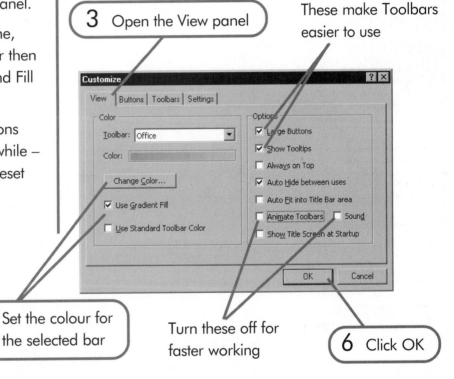

4 Set the colour for the selected bar

Turn these off for faster working

6 Click OK

Tip

If you want to use the AutoHide feature, you may find it best to locate the Toolbar on the left edge of the screen. You are less likely to activate anything in it accidentally there than at the right or bottom (close to the scroll bars) or at the top (close to the menu bar and control buttons).

Menus

The Office XP suite is huge and complex, but straightforward to use – at a basic level. (Mastery takes time!) A key factor in this ease of use is that – wherever possible – the same jobs are performed using the same buttons or menus. As there is a large core of common tasks, once you have got the hang of one application, you are on the way to learning the next.

Menus

Commands are grouped on menus, with only the more commonly-used ones visible at first. Browse through them to see the type of command to be found on each menu.

● An arrow to the right of an item leads to a submenu;

● If a menu item is followed by ... then selecting it opens up a dialog box where you specify details.

● If there is a [☒   ] at the bottom, click on it – or wait a few seconds – to open up the full menu.

If you use a 'hidden' command, it will be displayed on the menu for the rest of the working session. If you use the same 'hidden' command regularly, it will be added to the visible set.

❏ Mouse control

1 Click on a name to open a menu.

2 Point to an arrowed item to open its menu.

3 Click on a menu item to select it.

❏ Keyboard control

4 Hold down [Alt] and press the underlined letter to open a menu, then press an underlined letter to open a submenu or select a command, e.g. [Alt]+[I] then [P] then [H] selects Insert – Picture – Chart.

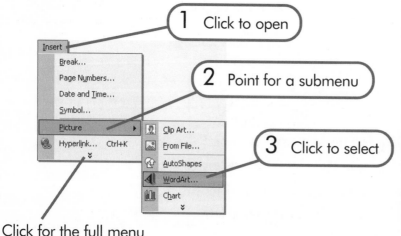

Click for the full menu

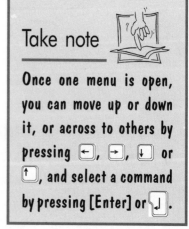

Take note

Once one menu is open, you can move up or down it, or across to others by pressing ←, →, ↓ or ↑, and select a command by pressing [Enter] or ↵.

8

Context menus

Like all modern Windows software, Office applications use context menus. These are opened by right-clicking on an item – a picture, cell, block of text, the background or whatever. The menus display those commands that are most commonly used with the selected item.

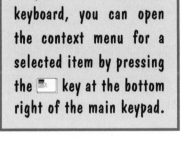

The context menu for a block of text in Word – this one draws applicable commands from the Edit, Format and Insert menus

The context menu for an object on a PowerPoint slide

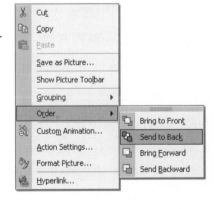

The context menu for an cell in an Excel worksheet

The context menu for a Journal entry in Outlook

Dialog boxes

If a menu command is followed by **...**, selecting it will open a dialog box. These are used where there are range of options or where the command needs you to enter additional information.

Some dialog boxes have several sets of options in them, each on a separate panel. These are identified by tabs at the top. Click on a tab to bring its panel to the front.

Most dialog boxes will have these buttons:

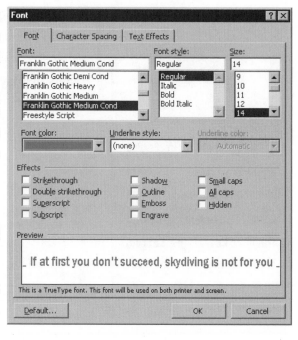

OK   fix your selections and entered data and close the box

Apply   fix the options set so far, but do not leave the box;

Cancel   to abandon your option settings;

Help   or **?** to get Help on items in the box.

Options may be set through:

Check boxes, where there are several options, and you can use as many as you like at the same time. ✔ in the box shows that the option has been selected.

These three are on

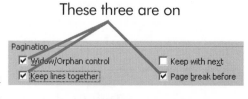

Radio buttons, which are used for either/or options. Only one of the set can be selected. The selected option is shown by a black blob in the middle.

This one please

Drop-down lists, recognised by a down arrow button to the right of a slot – click the button to open the list, and click on an item in the list to select.

Click here...

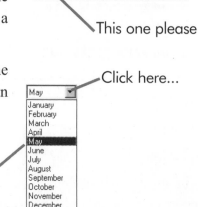

... to select from the list

The Task Pane

The Task Pane is a new feature of Office XP, and handles some of the operations that would otherwise be managed through dialog boxes. The advantage of the Task Pane is that it can remain open while you work so that you can perform a series of operations without having to reopen a dialog box each time.

When the Task Pane is open, you can switch between its functions by selecting from its drop-down menu.

You can open the Task Pane from the View menu

Use the drop-down menu to change the operation in the Task Pane

Back and Forward between the operations that you have used during the session

Click to close

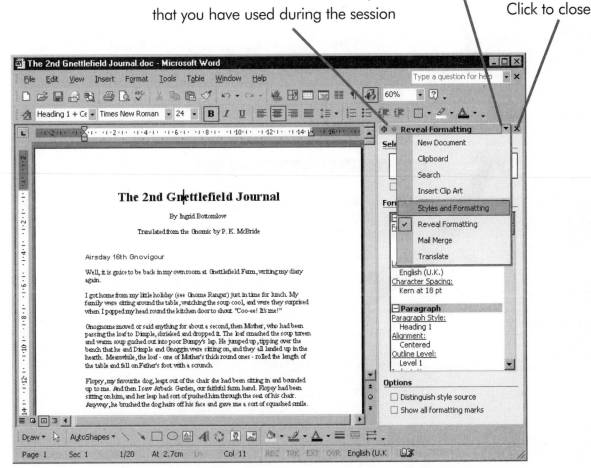

Custom menus

You may not want to customise menus straight away, but it is useful to know that it can be done. For instance, a *Close All* command might be useful if you regularly work with several documents open. You can add commands from any category onto any menu, though it helps to keep the same kind together.

Basic steps

1 On the Tools menu, select Customize...

2 Open the Commands panel.

3 Click on the menu to open it for editing.

4 Select a Category.

5 Find the Command that you want to add.

6 Drag it onto the menu.

Tip

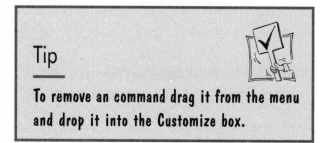

To remove an command drag it from the menu and drop it into the Customize box.

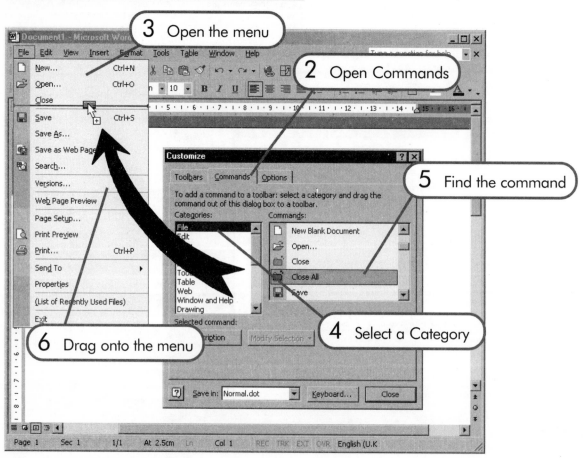

3 Open the menu

2 Open Commands

5 Find the command

6 Drag onto the menu

4 Select a Category

Basic steps

1 Open the Customize Commands panel from the Tools menu.

2 Select the menu item.

3 Click Modify Selection.

4 Point to Change Button Image and click on one to select it.

5 Click Close.

Menu item style

The Modify Selection option on the Customize box allows you to change the image, selection letter, grouping and other aspects of the appearance of menu items. Try changing the image – a good icon can help you find a command faster.

● You can only add images to simple commands – not to those that open submenus, or that are usually hidden.

● You can also change the [Alt] selection letter – indicated by '&' before it. To set a new selection letter, type '&' before it, and delete the existing '&'.

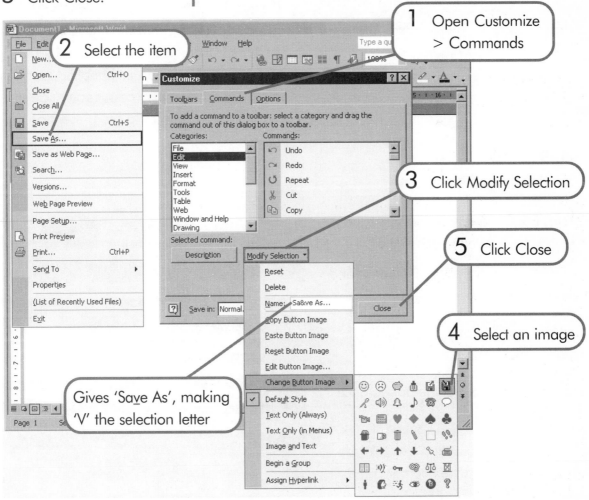

Toolbars

The buttons on the toolbars give quick and easy access to the more commonly-used commands. Each application has half a dozen or more toolbars, many of which – with variations – are found in all.

Some toolbars are open by default, but all can be displayed or removed as required. You can also add or remove buttons from any bar, see the next page.

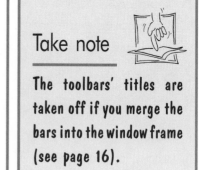

Take note

The toolbars' titles are taken off if you merge the bars into the window frame (see page 16).

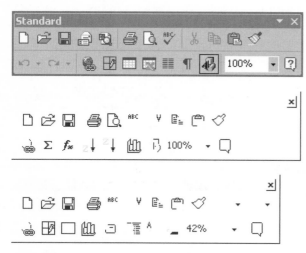

The Standard toolbars from Word (top), Excel (middle) and PowerPoint (bottom), hold the buttons for most commonly-used commands. Those for file handling, printing, editing, Internet access, zoom (screen magnification) and Help are present on all three toolbars.

Word, Excel and PowerPoint have these, though their contents vary slightly.

Formatting sets the style, alignment and layout of text.

Drawing has line and shape tools for creating diagrams.

Picture lets you control the appearance of an inserted picture.

Web turns the application into a Web browser for surfing the Internet.

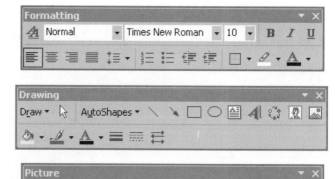

Selecting toolbars

- Selecting toolbars

1 Open the View menu and select Toolbars...

Or

2 Right-click on any toolbar to open the same Toolbars menu.

3 Click a name to turn its display on ▣ or off.

- Customizing

4 From the Toolbars menu, pick Customize.

5 On the Options panel, adjust the display to suit yourself.

If you find toolbars useful – and you will – you can have more on screen than just the default ones. But don't overdo it. Every toolbar you add reduces the amount of visible working space!

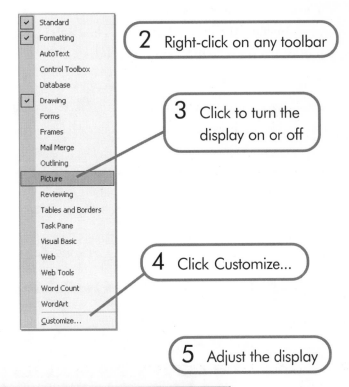

2 Right-click on any toolbar

3 Click to turn the display on or off

4 Click Customize...

5 Adjust the display

Some toolbars are not on the Toolbars menu, but all are in the Toolbars tab – add or remove any from here

ScreenTips remind you what the buttons do

Do you like to use keyboard shortcuts?

Animation is a pain in the eyes – ignore it

Large buttons are easier to see, but take up more space

15

Placing toolbars

Button toolbars can be merged into the window frame, or allowed to 'float' on the document area. The position and size of floating toolbars can be adjusted at any time.

● Those bars that you want to use all of the time are probably best fitted into the frame. They will go into any part of the frame – top, bottom or sides.

● Those that are only wanted for the occasional job – e.g. *Drawing* for creating an illustration – can be brought up as needed, and floated in a convenient place.

Basic steps

1 Point to the title bar or to the lines at the start of the toolbar.

2 Drag the toolbar, pushing it off the edge if you want to merge it into the frame.

3 Release the mouse button.

4 Drag on an edge or corner to resize a floating toolbar.

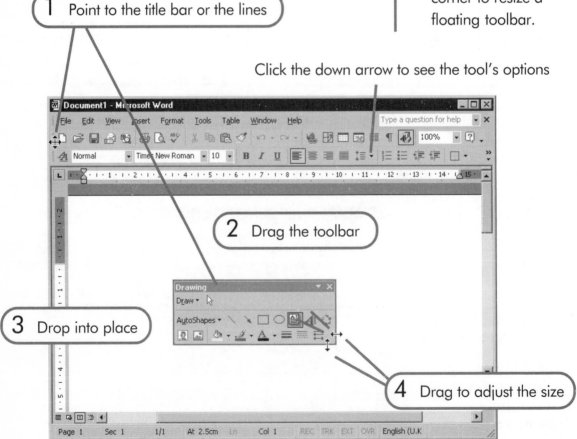

1 Point to the title bar or the lines

Click the down arrow to see the tool's options

2 Drag the toolbar

3 Drop into place

4 Drag to adjust the size

Basic steps

1 Click the arrowhead at the end of a toolbar in the frame.

Or

2 Click the white arrow-head on a floating toolbar's title bar.

3 Click Add or Remove Buttons then the toolbar's name.

4 Click on a button name to turn it on or off.

5 Click anywhere to end.

Adding and removing buttons

Every toolbar has an Add or Remove Buttons command which will display the full set of buttons for that toolbar. A simple click will then add or remove a button from the toolbar. At some point, spend a few minutes adjusting the toolbars so that you have easy access to the tools you use most, without the clutter of rarely-used tools.

Take note

You can also add or remove toolbar buttons using the Customize tab – just drag them onto the toolbar instead of a menu.

1 Click the arrowhead

3 Click Add or Remove Buttons then the toolbar name

4 Click to turn on or off

5 Click elsewhere

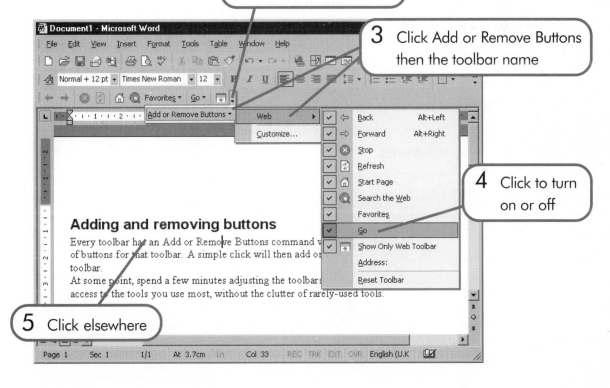

Summary

- ❑ Office programs can be run from the Start menu, Desktop shortcuts or the Shortcut Bar – pick the approach that best suits your way of working.

- ❑ The Shortcut Bar can be placed anywhere on the screen, and can be set to hide itself when not in use.

- ❑ You can add buttons to the Shortcut Bar, and link other toolbars onto it.

- ❑ All commands can be accessed through the menus, and all the common ones through the toolbars.

- ❑ Many of the items on the menus and toolbars are the same in all Office applications.

- ❑ Dialog boxes are used for setting options and entering data.

- ❑ Some of the more common operations are run through the Task Pane. This can be left open to run a series of operations.

- ❑ Commands can be added to or removed from menus.

- ❑ The Standard and Formatting toolbars are normally displayed. Other ones can be brought onto the screen as and when they are needed.

2 Filing

New documents

You can start a new document from the Office Shortcut bar as well as from within applications. The document can be based on a 'blank', or on a template or wizard. These can both help you to create attractive, effective documents, spreadsheets and presentations, but approach them from different ways.

First, here's how to start a new document when you don't have its application running already.

Basic steps

1 Click the New document button on the Shortcut bar.

Or

2 Open the Start menu and select New Office Document.

3 Switch to the appropriate panel.

4 Select a template or wizard.

5 Click [OK].

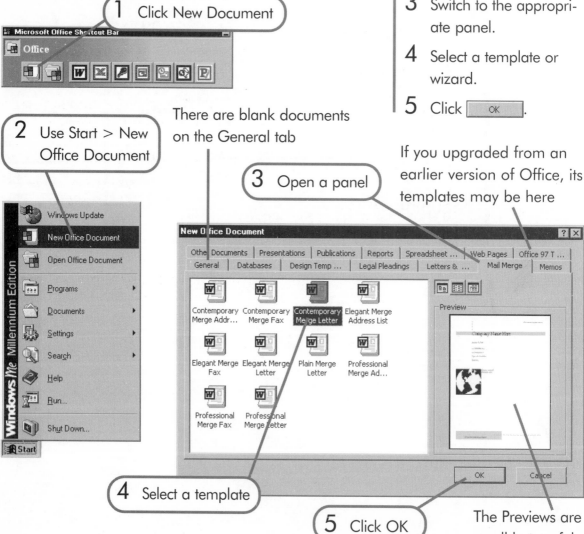

1 Click New Document

2 Use Start > New Office Document

There are blank documents on the General tab

3 Open a panel

If you upgraded from an earlier version of Office, its templates may be here

4 Select a template

5 Click OK

The Previews are small but useful

20

Basic steps

1 Pull down the File menu and select New.

2 Select the type of blank document.

Or

3 Click a Template link.

4 Select a template or wizard.

5 Click [OK].

Tip

Click to start a new blank document.

Take note

Templates and Wizards are covered on pages 36 to 41. The examples are from Word, but the same techniques are used in all applications.

New documents in the Task Pane

When you first start up an Office application, you will normally see the New Document display in the Task Pane. The same display appears in response to the **File > New** command.

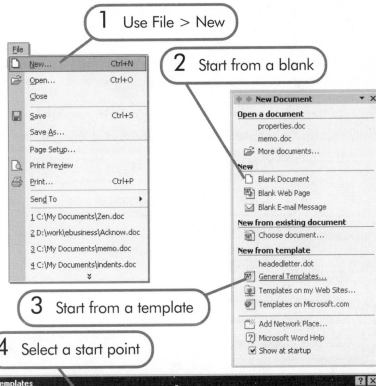

1 Use File > New

2 Start from a blank

3 Start from a template

4 Select a start point

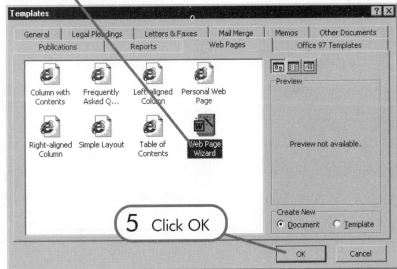

5 Click OK

21

Opening files

There are several ways to open an existing Office file. Which way to take depends largely upon where you are when you start:

- If you have not yet opened the application, use Open on the Office Shortcut bar or select Open Office Document from the Start menu.

- If the application is open, and you want an old file, use the File Open command or the 🗁 button.

- If the application is open and the file has been used recently, open the File menu and select it from the set at the bottom of the menu.

1 Click Open on the Shortcut bar

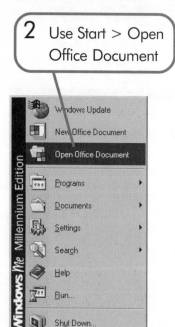

2 Use Start > Open Office Document

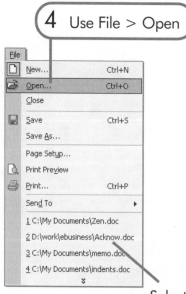

4 Use File > Open

Select a recently used file from the bottom of the File menu

❑ From Windows

1 Click 🗗 on the Shortcut bar.

Or

2 Click Start and select Open Office Document.

❑ From an application

3 Click 🗁 on the standard Toolbar.

Or

4 Open the File menu and select Open.

5 Choose a Look in area – e.g. *History* or *My Documents*.

6 Open the folder if necessary.

7 Set the Files of type to the appropriate type.

8 If you want details of the files, click 🔲 and select the Preview or Properties view.

9 Select the file and click Open ▾.

22

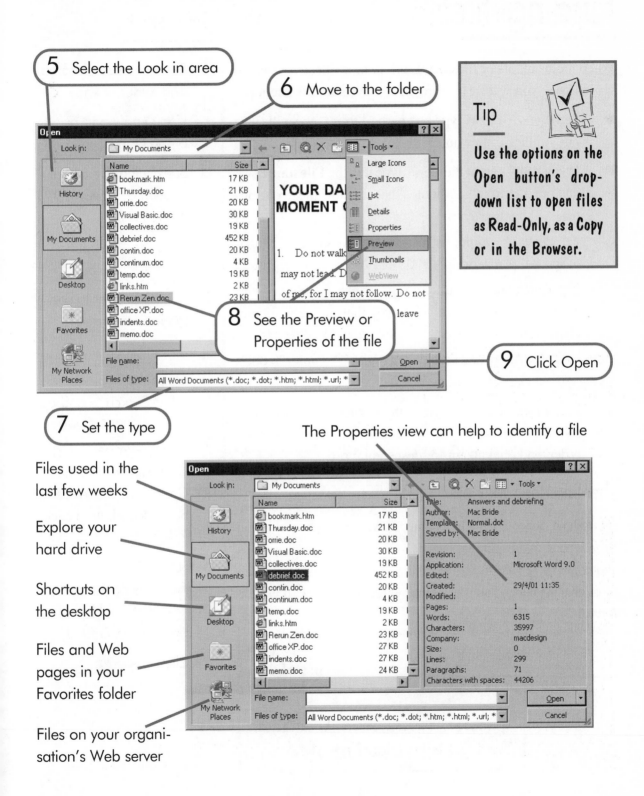

5 Select the Look in area

6 Move to the folder

8 See the Preview or Properties of the file

7 Set the type

9 Click Open

The Properties view can help to identify a file

Files used in the last few weeks

Explore your hard drive

Shortcuts on the desktop

Files and Web pages in your Favorites folder

Files on your organi-sation's Web server

Finding files

When there are lots of files in a **Look in** area, it can be hard to spot the one you want. Here are three ways simplify the job.

- Setting the **Files of type** box to the correct type will filter out swathes of unwanted stuff.

- If you know part of the name, type it in the **File name** box and press **[Enter]**. Only files that contains those characters will be displayed:

  e.g. '*memo*' would list '*memo* to boss.doc', '29june *memo*.txt', '*memo*ry costs.xls'

  If you are unsure about some characters, fill the gap with an asterisk (*) – this is a 'wildcard', that can stand for any characters:

  e.g. '*chap*2*' would find '*chap*ter2.doc', '*chap*ter20.doc', '*chap*el choir May 12.txt'

- In the Details display, you can list files by Name, Size, Type or Date – just click on the header to list in ascending order, and click again for descending order.

The Search panel

If you have forgotten a file's name, or where you stored it, the Search panel is the answer. This will look through the properties and contents of files to find matching words. It can also search through subfolders – so if it's somewhere on the disk, it will be found!

> **Tip**
>
> **When you type a name, ignore the extension. That is set in the Files of type slot.**

1 Select the Look in area and folder, if known.

2 If you know part or all of the Name, enter it.

3 Specify the File type if known, otherwise set this to All files.

4 Click the ▦▾ button and select Details.

5 Click a header to sort the list into order.

❏ If it isn't found...

6 Open the Tools menu, select Search... and go to the Advanced tab.

7 Select a Property, e.g. *Contents* and set the Condition and Value to be matched, then click Add .

8 Set the Search in: locations and the Results should be: file types, if required.

9 Click Search .

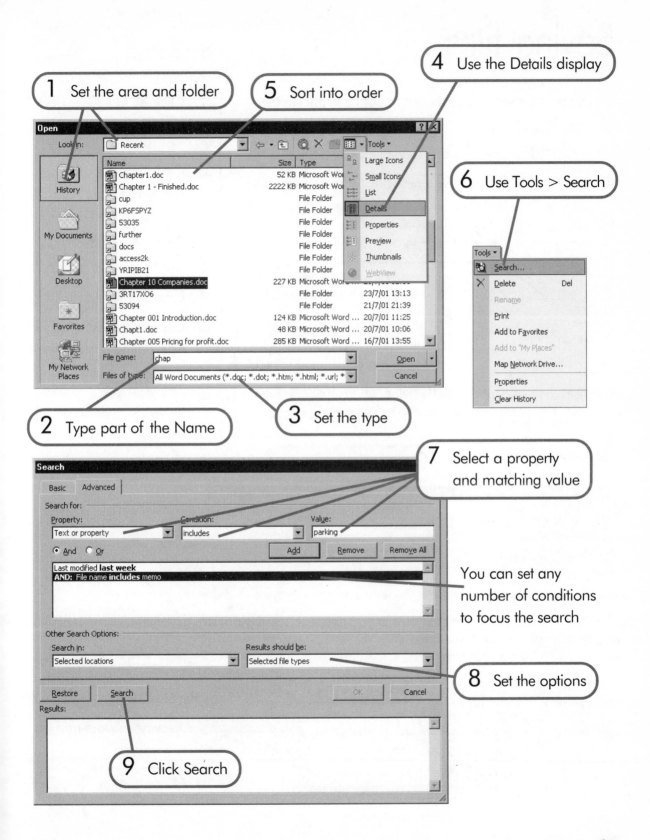

1 Set the area and folder

5 Sort into order

4 Use the Details display

6 Use Tools > Search

Open

Look in: Recent

Name	Size	Type
Chapter1.doc	52 KB	Microsoft Wor
Chapter 1 - Finished.doc	2222 KB	Microsoft Wor
cup		File Folder
KP6FSPYZ		File Folder
53035		File Folder
further		File Folder
docs		File Folder
access2k		File Folder
YRIPIB21		File Folder
Chapter 10 Companies.doc	227 KB	Microsoft Wor
3RT17XO6		File Folder	23/7/01 13:13
53094		File Folder	21/7/01 21:39
Chapter 001 Introduction.doc	124 KB	Microsoft Word ...	20/7/01 11:25
Chapt1.doc	48 KB	Microsoft Word ...	20/7/01 10:06
Chapter 005 Pricing for profit.doc	285 KB	Microsoft Word ...	16/7/01 13:55

Large Icons
Small Icons
List
Details
Properties
Preview
Thumbnails
WebView

Tools ▾
- Search...
- Delete   Del
- Rename
- Print
- Add to Favorites
- Add to "My Places"
- Map Network Drive...
- Properties
- Clear History

History
My Documents
Desktop
Favorites
My Network Places

File name: chap
Files of type: All Word Documents (*.doc; *.dot; *.htm; *.html; *.url; *

Open
Cancel

2 Type part of the Name

3 Set the type

Search

Basic | Advanced

Search for:

Property: Text or property

Condition: includes

Value: parking

○ And ○ Or   Add   Remove   Remove All

Last modified **last week**
AND: File name **includes** memo

7 Select a property and matching value

You can set any number of conditions to focus the search

Other Search Options:

Search in: Selected locations

Results should be: Selected file types

8 Set the options

Restore   Search   OK   Cancel

Results:

9 Click Search

Saving files

There are two file-saving routines in Office applications.

- **Save** is used to save an existing file after editing – just click 🖫 or open the **File** menu and select **Save**.

- **Save As** is used to save a new file, or to save an existing file with a new name or in a new folder – see the steps.

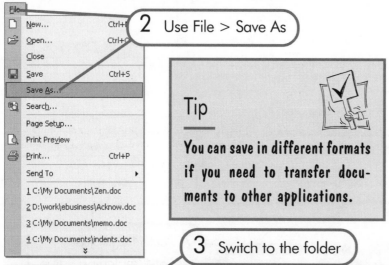

2 Use File > Save As

Tip

You can save in different formats if you need to transfer documents to other applications.

3 Switch to the folder

4 Give a name

5 Set the file type?

6 Click Save

See opposite

Set passwords

When saving as HTML

Smaller files for transfer by disk or e-mail

Use when updating files

Basic steps

1 Click 🖫 to save a new file.

Or

2 Open the File menu and select Save As to save a file with a new name or location.

3 Set the Save in folder.

4 Enter the Filename.

5 Change the Save as type setting if required.

6 Click ▭ Save ▭.

7 Return to editing, or exit, as desired.

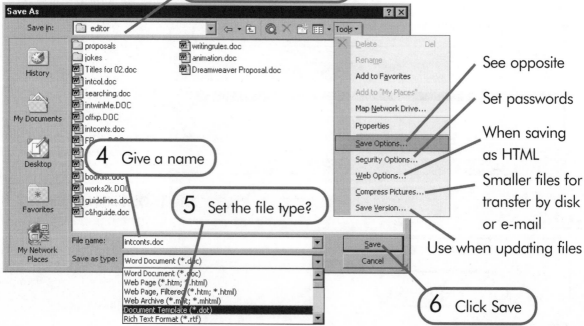

Save options

Tools – General Options on the **Save** panel opens an extensive Options panel in Word and a simpler one in Excel. PowerPoint allows no options for individual files, though you can set defaults on the **Save** tab of the **Tools – Options** panel. The key options are those which protect the file:

Password to open, prevents all unauthorised access;

Password to modify allows anyone to read it, but only the password holder can save it, with the same name;

Read recommended sets Read Only as the default mode for opening the file.

If you have any doubts about the PC's reliability, turn on Always create Backup copy

PowerPoint also lets you Embed True Type fonts, to ensure that the document looks the same on any PC

Save AutoRecover guards against lost work – set a reasonable interval

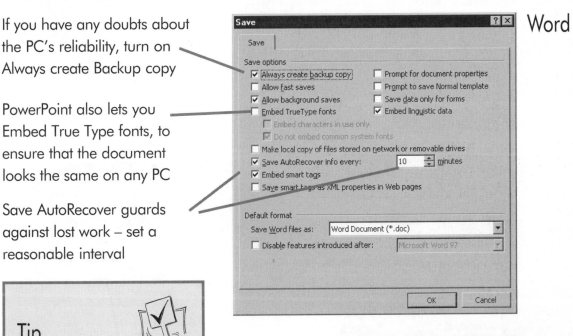

Word

Excel

File properties

All Office XP files have Properties panels which contain information about the nature of the file. These can be viewed when opening files (see page 22) and searched in the Search routine (see page 24).

- The **General** tab holds the basic details of the file – location, size, date saved, etc.;

- The basic information on the **Summary** tab is produced by Office XP – fill in the blanks as required and tick **Save preview picture** if wanted. The Preview shows the first page – it can be displayed in the Open panel (see page 23).

- On the **Statistics** tab, the Words count is useful for students, journalists or anyone else working to a set limit;

- The **Contents** tab lists the headings in a Word document, slide titles in a presentation, or sheets in an Excel book;

- The **Custom** tab can hold other details of the document – this is for advanced users only!

Basic steps

1 Open the File menu and select Properties.

2 Switch to the Summary panel.

3 Enter information as required – the Subject and Keywords will be useful in future Finds.

4 Turn on Save Preview Picture if this will help to identify the file later.

5 Click OK.

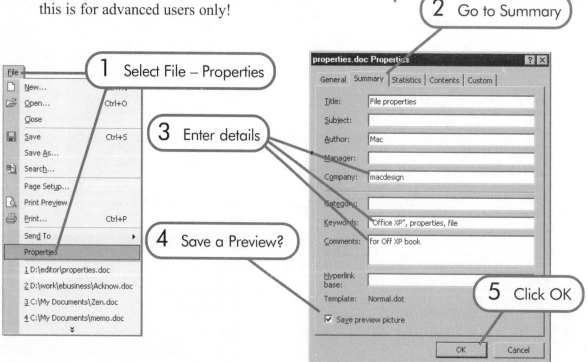

28

Take note

You must save the file (again) after filling in the Properties, to save the information.

The Contents are generated only if the Save Preview picture option is checked.

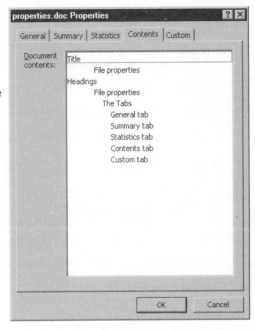

On the Statistics panel, don't believe the Total editing time figure, it is simply how long the file was open!

To add Custom information, select the Name and Type, enter the Value and click Add.

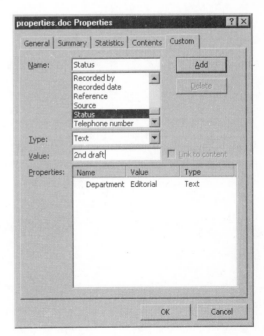

Summary

❑ Files can be opened from the Shortcut bar or from within applications.

❑ There are templates and wizards available to simplify setting up new documents.

❑ The Search facility helps you to track down files if you have forgotten their names or folders.

❑ When saving files for the first time, you must specify a folder and filename through the Save As dialog box. Resaving simply takes a click on the Save button.

❑ When saving a file, if you save its Preview, you will make it easier to find it when you want to open it in the future.

❑ A file's Properties panel can hold summary data and a description of the file.

3 Word

Introducing Word

Word can be used to produce just about any text-based document – letters, flyers, Web pages, reports, newsletters, even books (complete with contents, index and footnotes)!

For the most part it is remarkably easy to use – and the trickier operations are those which most people will rarely need. To make things even easier, Word is equipped with dozens of templates and wizards which provide the style, layout and suggested contents for a wide range of documents.

The Word window

The bulk of the space is taken up, of course, by the working area where you type your text, and insert graphics and other objects to create your documents. Around this area are:

- The **Title bar**, showing the name of the document, and carrying the usual Minimize, Maximize/Restore and Close application buttons.

- The **Menu bar**, giving you access to the full command set. At the far right is the Close document button ⊠ – click to close the document, but keep Word active. If you open a second document (in a new window) this Close button is not present – when you close a second document, you also close its window.

- The **toolbars** – normally just the Standard and Formatting toolbars, but others can be displayed as required. The toolbars are usually at the top or bottom of the working area, but can be moved or floated (see page 16).

- The **scroll bars**, used for moving around your document. At the bottom of the right scroll bar are buttons for switching between pages; and at the the left of the bottom bar are four buttons for changing the view.

Take note

If you know what you want to say, Word will help you to say it better, and give a professional gloss to your documents.

Take note

When you first start Word, the Task pane is open. This closes automatically when you begin work on a document, but can be opened again (from the View menu) if needed.

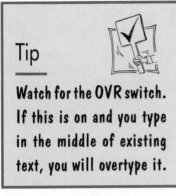

Tip

Watch for the OVR switch. If this is on and you type in the middle of existing text, you will overtype it.

- The **rulers**, showing the margins, indents and tabs. These are not present in some views (see page 34).

- The **Status bar** helps to keep you informed. It shows where you are in the document, what language the spell checker (see page 108) is using, and the state of various switches.

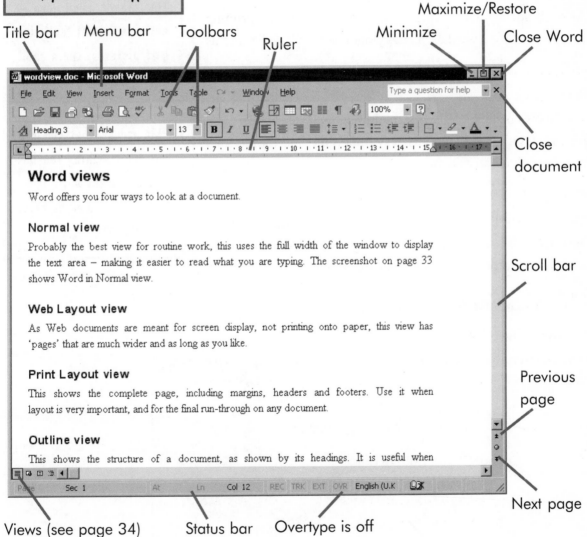

Title bar · Menu bar · Toolbars · Ruler · Minimize · Maximize/Restore · Close Word · Close document · Scroll bar · Previous page · Next page · Views (see page 34) · Status bar · Overtype is off

Word views

Word offers you four ways to look at a document.

Normal view

Probably the best view for routine work, this uses the full width of the window to display the text area – making it easier to read what you are typing. The screenshot on page 33 shows Word in Normal view.

Web Layout view

As Web documents are meant for screen display, not printing onto paper, this view has 'pages' that are much wider and as long as you like.

Print Layout view

This shows the complete page, including margins, headers and footers. Use it when layout is very important, and for the final run-through on any document.

Outline view

This shows the structure of a document, as shown by its headings. It is useful when

Word views

Word offers you four ways to look at a document.

Normal view
Probably the best view for routine work, this uses the full width of the window to display the text area – making it easier to read what you are typing. The screenshot on page 33 shows Word in Normal view.

Web Layout view
As Web documents are meant for screen display, not printing onto paper, this view has 'pages' that are much wider and as long as you like.

Print Layout view
This shows the complete page, including margins, headers and footers. Use it when layout is very important, and for the final run-through on any document.

Outline view
This shows the structure of a document, as shown by its headings. It is useful when planning a new document, and simplifies reorganising long, multi-page ones.

Changing views

To switch between views, use the buttons at the bottom left of the screen, or the options on the View menu.

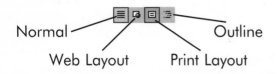

Normal Outline

Web Layout Print Layout

Take note

You can do most jobs — edit and format text, insert pictures, run a spell check, and many more — in all four views.

This means that you can put the finishing touches to a document while looking at it in **Web** or **Print Layout** view.

34

Web Layout view

Print Layout view

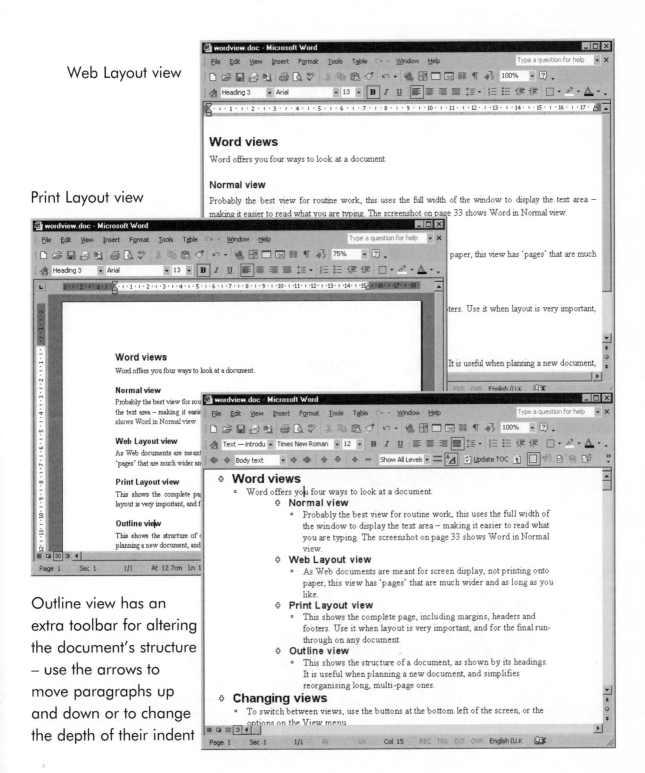

Outline view has an
extra toolbar for altering
the document's structure
– use the arrows to
move paragraphs up
and down or to change
the depth of their indent

Documents and templates

All documents start from some kind of template which sets up the basic design. Even the 'blank document' is a template, though this simply sets the page size and the fonts for the normal and heading text. Other templates have more elaborate design features and suggestions for content and layout of the items to include in the new document.

Basic steps

1 If the Task pane is not visible, open it from the View menu.

2 Select Blank Document or Blank Web Page.

Or

3 Select General Templates…

4 At the Templates dialog box, select a tab.

Tip

You can also start a new blank document with the New button or the File > New command.

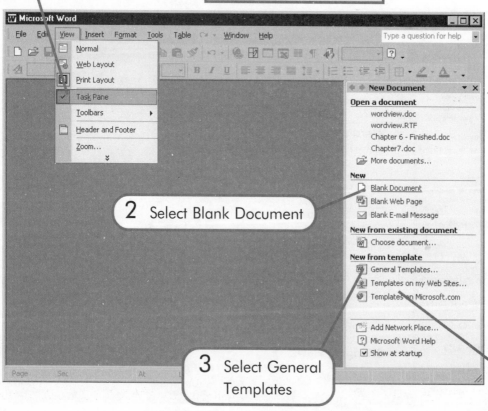

1 Open the Task Pane

2 Select Blank Document

3 Select General Templates

More templates can be found online

5 Click on a template to see its preview.

6 When you find a suitable template, click OK.

7 Click into the prompts and replace them with your own details.

If you had earlier Office versions, their templates may be available

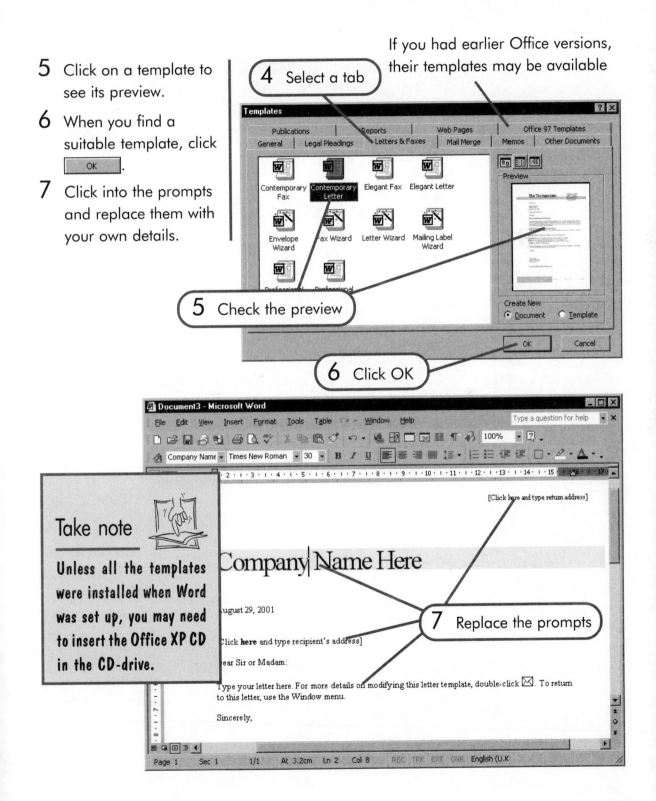

4 Select a tab

5 Check the preview

6 Click OK

7 Replace the prompts

Take note

Unless all the templates were installed when Word was set up, you may need to insert the **Office XP CD** in the CD-drive.

Sample letter based on the Contemporary Letter template

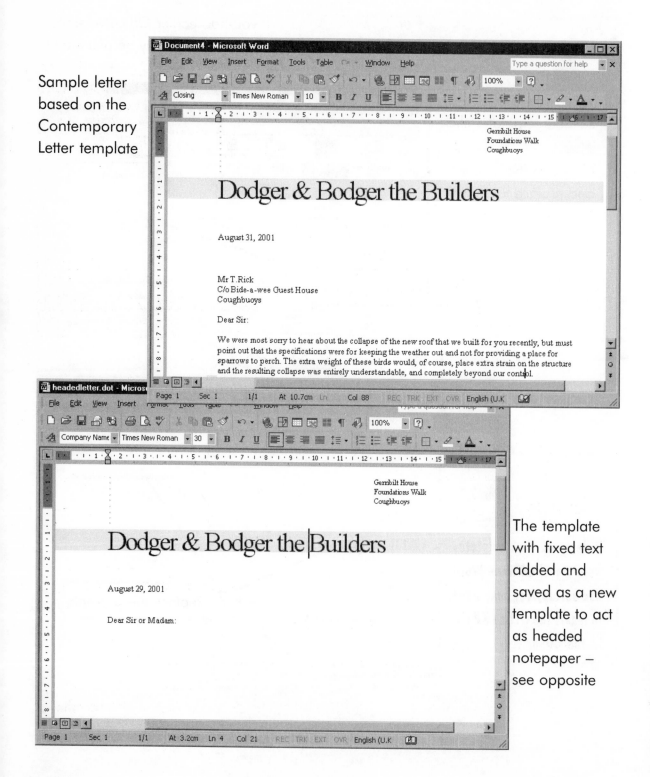

The template with fixed text added and saved as a new template to act as headed notepaper – see opposite

Making your own templates

1 Starting from a template or blank document, enter the fixed text and other items.

2 Open the File menu and select Save As...

3 From the Save as type drop-down list select *Document Template*.

4 Enter a filename.

5 Click [Save].

❑ Your template can be opened from the New dialog box.

This is so easy, and so useful, that you should explore it early on in your use of Word. You can create your own templates for everything from headed notepaper to draft contracts. All you need to do is set up a document with a suitable design and layout and all the fixed information, but leave out any specific details – the name of the person, the quote for the job, the text of the letter, and so forth – then save it the right way.

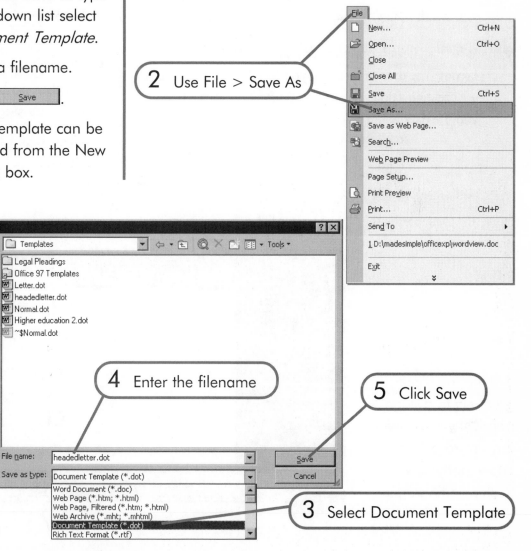

2 Use File > Save As

4 Enter the filename

5 Click Save

3 Select Document Template

39

Document wizards

In amongst the ordinary templates are a number of wizards which offer alternative ways to start new documents. They tend to be used where there are more optional elements – setting them through a wizard means that the basic document is closer to what you want than a normal template could be.

Wizards are simple to use, and all work along the same lines.

● Where there are alternatives, click the button by the one you want:

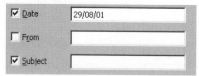

● Where an item is optional, tick the box to include it in the layout. The data to be displayed should be entered if you are creating a document, but left blank if this is a template and the data is not a fixed item.

Here, for example, is the Memo wizard in action.

You can also work through the wizard by clicking the blocks to go direct to a stage – handy if you've used the wizard before and know that you want to skip some stages.

1 At the New dialog box, select the wizard you require.

2 Work through the wizard, setting the options or entering details at the prompts.

3 Click `Next >` to move on to the next stage.

4 Click `< Back` if you need to go back to the previous stage.

5 Click `Finish` when done.

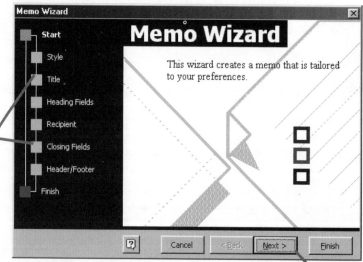

3 Click Next

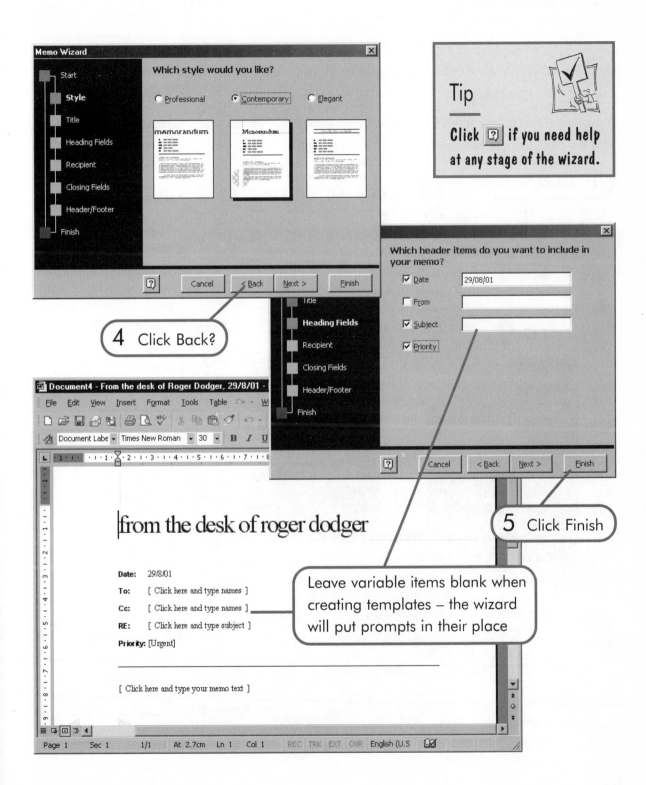

Memo Wizard

Which style would you like?

○ Professional ● Contemporary ○ Elegant

- Start
- **Style**
- Title
- Heading Fields
- Recipient
- Closing Fields
- Header/Footer
- Finish

Cancel < Back Next > Finish

Tip

Click ❓ if you need help at any stage of the wizard.

Which header items do you want to include in your memo?

☑ Date 29/08/01
☐ From
☑ Subject
☑ Priority

- Title
- **Heading Fields**
- Recipient
- Closing Fields
- Header/Footer
- Finish

Cancel < Back Next > Finish

4 Click Back?

5 Click Finish

Document4 - From the desk of Roger Dodger, 29/8/01 -

File Edit View Insert Format Tools Table

Document Labe Times New Roman 30 **B** *I* U

from the desk of roger dodger

Date: 29/8/01
To: [Click here and type names]
Cc: [Click here and type names]
RE: [Click here and type subject]
Priority: [Urgent]

[Click here and type your memo text]

Leave variable items blank when creating templates – the wizard will put prompts in their place

Page 1 Sec 1 1/1 At 2.7cm Ln 1 Col 1 REC TRK EXT OVR English (U.S

Columns

Word's layout facilities are almost as good as you will find in dedicated DTP (desktop publishing) software – its handling of columns is a good example.

You can set text in two or three columns, of the same or different widths, over the whole document or a selected part.

Basic steps

1 Select the text to set if only part is to be in columns.

2 Open the Format menu and select Columns...

3 Select the closest Preset design.

4 Clear Equal spacing and adjust the Width or Spacing if wanted.

5 Tick Line between if required.

6 Set the Apply to option.

7 Click OK .

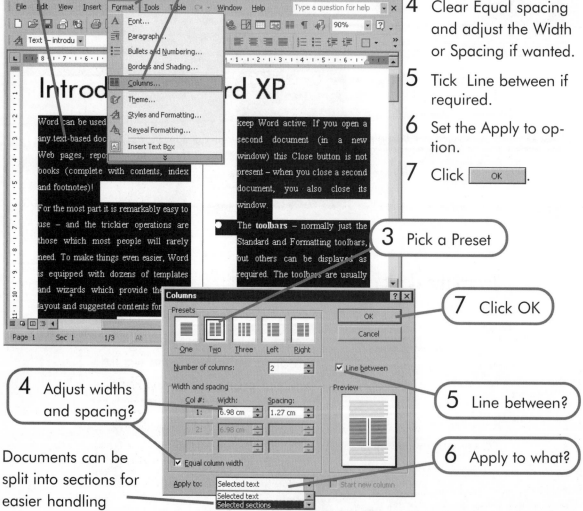

1 Select the text?

2 Use Format > Columns

3 Pick a Preset

7 Click OK

4 Adjust widths and spacing?

5 Line between?

6 Apply to what?

Documents can be split into sections for easier handling

Basic steps

1 Open the View menu and select Header and Footer.

2 Click into the header.

3 Open the Insert menu and select Page Numbers, Date and Time or an Autotext entry.

4 Add any other text then format as usual.

5 Repeat for the footer.

6 Click into the main text to return to editing.

Headers and footers

Headers and footers are a useful addition to documents of more than one page. At the very least, you can use them to display the page numbers, but the title, date, filename and other information can also be displayed here.

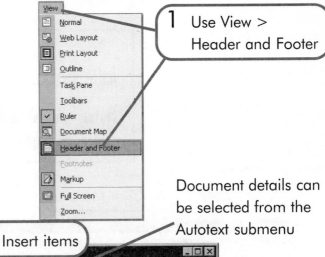

1 Use View > Header and Footer

Document details can be selected from the Autotext submenu

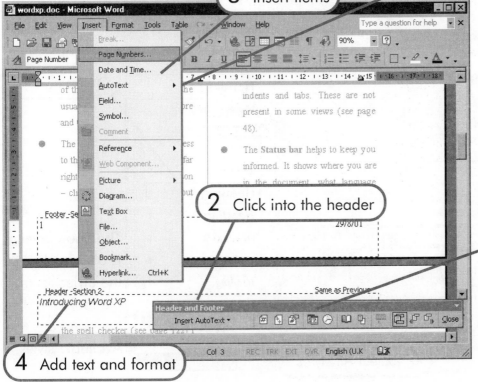

3 Insert items

2 Click into the header

Items can also be inserted from the Header and Footer toolbar

4 Add text and format

Styles

A *style* is a combination of font, size, alignment and indent options. Word has a range of pre-defined styles, and you can modify these or add your own. Applying a style is a matter of a couple of clicks; creating a new style is almost as simple.

Basic steps

❑ Applying a style

1 Select the paragraph.

2 Pick a style from the drop-down Styles list.

or

3 Click More... to open the styles list in the Task Pane.

4 In the Show box, select All styles.

5 Pick from the long list.

Take note

Styles always apply to whole paragraphs.

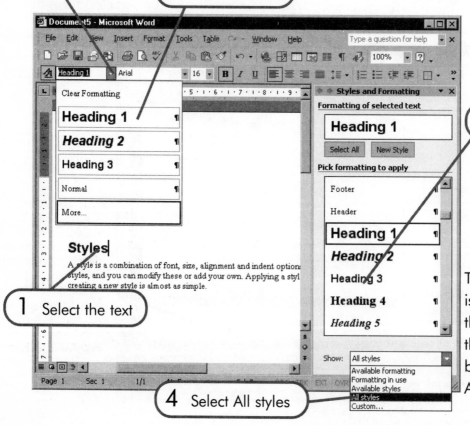

2 Pick a style

3 Click More...

5 Pick a style

1 Select the text

4 Select All styles

The Show setting is also applied to the Styles list in the toolbar – it's best kept at Available styles

- ❑ Modifying a style
- 1 Open Styles and Formatting in the Task Pane.
- 2 Pick a style.
- 3 Click its down arrow and select Modify…
- 4 Edit the main format settings if required.
- 5 For more extensive changes, click the Format button and select an aspect to open its dialog box.
- 6 Click [OK].
- ❑ Creating a style
- 7 At the Style dialog box, click [New Style].
- 8 Type in a Name then follow steps 3 to 6.

Take note

For more on formatting, see Chapter 6, Working with text.

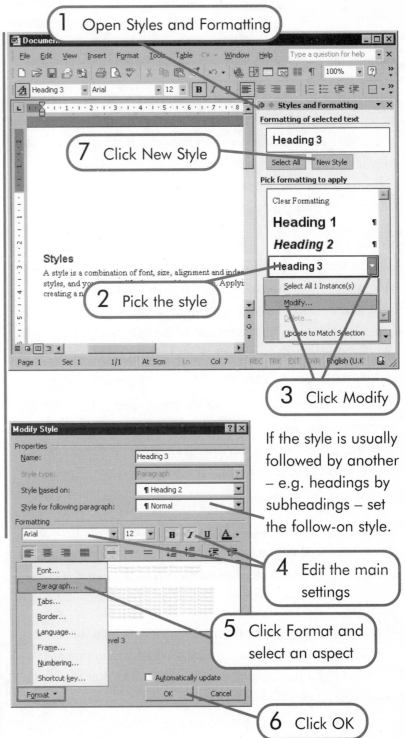

1 Open Styles and Formatting

7 Click New Style

2 Pick the style

3 Click Modify

If the style is usually followed by another – e.g. headings by subheadings – set the follow-on style.

4 Edit the main settings

5 Click Format and select an aspect

6 Click OK

Styles

A style is a combination of font, size, alignment and inde... styles, and yo... creating a n...

Page Setup

If you are creating anything other than routine letters and memos, the Page Setup may well need changing.

Paper size

You will need to change the size if you are printing on envelopes or unusual paper, and should always check it when working from a template, which may have been set up for US paper size. Use this tab also to set the orientation – upright (Portrait) or sideways (Landscape).

Setting margins

Use the Margins tab to adjust the space around the printed area. Margins should not be too small – printers can't reach the very edge of the paper and you need some white space around any text. Sometimes a slight reduction of the margins will give you a better printout. There is little more irritating than a couple of odd lines of text or a tiny block of data on a separate sheet.

If you are printing both sides of the paper, book-style, tick the Mirror margins box. If they are to be ring-bound, widen the inner margin or set the gutter (the space inside the inner margin) to allow for the hidden paper.

Paper source

This rarely needs attention. You might perhaps want to turn off the defaults so that you can manually feed in individual sheets of card or special paper, without emptying the paper tray.

Layout

This needs attention with large documents that have been divided into sections – you can set where each section starts – and where you have headers and footers, and don't want the same ones on every page.

Basic steps

1 Open the File menu and select Page Setup.

2 On the Margins tab, use the buttons to adjust the margins or enter new values.

3 Set the Orientation – *Portrait* or *Landscape*.

4 If required, turn on Mirror margins or 2 pages per sheet.

5 On the Paper tab, pick the Paper size.

6 On the Layout tab, set the Section start and Header and Footer options for large or multi-section documents, if appropriate.

7 Click OK.

Tip

The Preview on the Page Setup panels gives an idea of the printing area. To see how the document will look, use Print Preview.

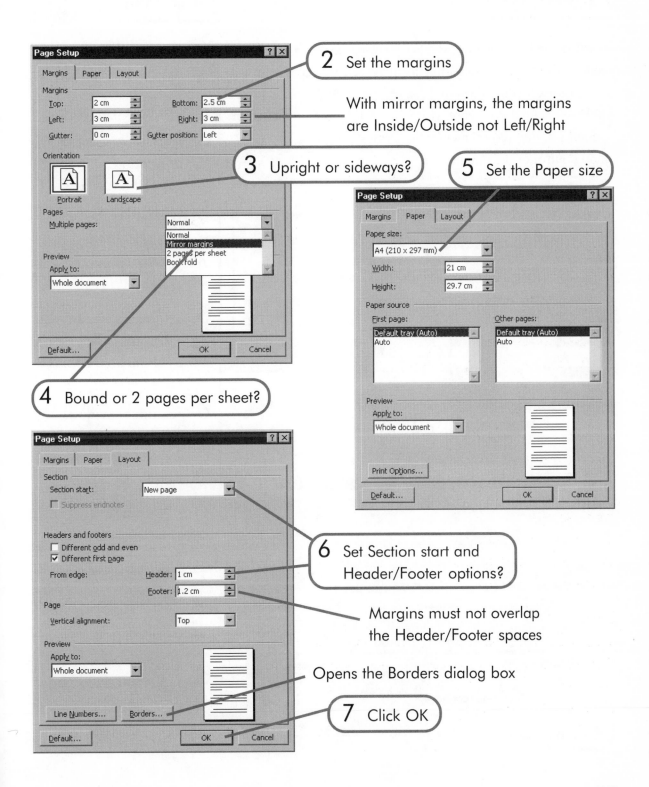

2 Set the margins

With mirror margins, the margins are Inside/Outside not Left/Right

3 Upright or sideways?

5 Set the Paper size

4 Bound or 2 pages per sheet?

6 Set Section start and Header/Footer options?

Margins must not overlap the Header/Footer spaces

Opens the Borders dialog box

7 Click OK

Printing

Word documents are (normally) page-based from the start, leading to a simple transition from screen to paper. With a straightforward document of just a few pages, the 'instant print' approach should do nicely. If you have longer documents, or special printing requirements, the Print dialog box gives you good control of the output.

❑ Instant print

1 Click 🖨.

❑ Controlled printing

2 If you only want to print part of a page, select the text first.

3 Open the File menu and select Print.

4 Set the range of pages to print.

5 Set the Copies number – turn on Collate to print multiple copies in sorted sets.

6 For double-sided printing, set the Print first to Odd pages then to Even pages.

7 Click [OK].

Tip

If you have a problem, first check that the printer is on and loaded with paper!

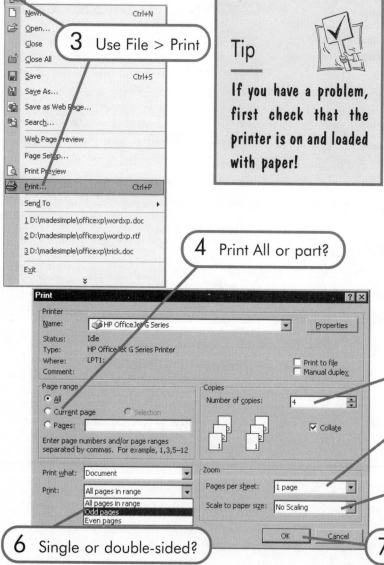

3 Use File > Print

4 Print All or part?

5 How many copies?

Small pages can be printed several to a sheet

Scale up or down to fit on different sized paper

6 Single or double-sided?

7 Click OK

48

Print Preview

Tip

If you have an odd few lines on the last page, click Shrink to fit. This tries to fit the document onto one less page.

If you work in Print Layout view, you can see – as you create the document – how it will fit on paper. By dropping the Zoom level down to Whole page or Two pages, you can get a better impression of the overall layout of the document.

Print Preview lets you view more pages – as thumbnails – at a time, has a Zoom tool which you can use to jump between 100% and the preview size, and shows the headers and footers more clearly. When previewing, you can still adjust font sizes, line spacing or the size and position of objects to get a better balanced page – all the normal menu commands are available and toolbars can be opened as needed.

Multiple pages   Ruler (on/off)   Shrink to fit

One page   Zoom level   Full screen (removes frame and menu bar)

Print

Magnifier (turn off to get editing pointer)

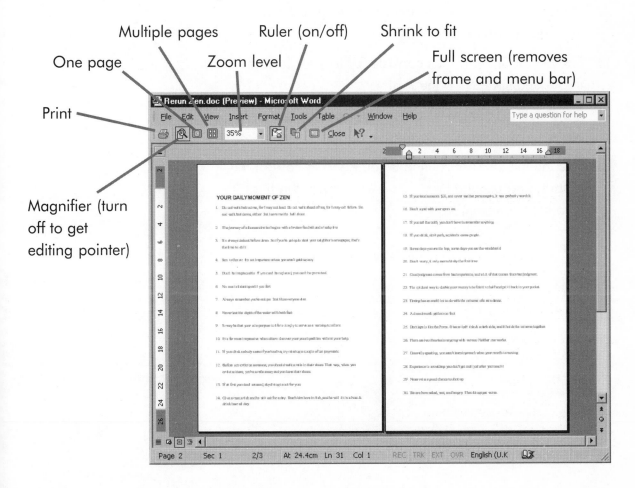

Summary

❑ Word can handle large and complex text-based jobs if required, but for straightforward work is exceptionally easy to use.

❑ Use the Normal view when creating a document, switching to the Web or Print layout views to check its layout, or to Outline view to reorganise paragraphs more easily.

❑ New documents can be started from scratch, or from a basic design set up by a template or wizard.

❑ Selected paragraphs can be set in columns.

❑ Headers and footers can be added to give fixed information on all pages.

❑ The use of Styles brings consistency to your formatting – and speeds up the job!

❑ If the output is anything other than A4 single sheets, use the Page Setup to define the layout.

❑ Use the File > Print routine if you need to control the output, and use the Print Preview to check the final layout before printing.

4 Excel

Introducing Excel

When spreadsheets first appeared, they were simply grids of cells into which text, numbers and formulae could be written. They have come a long way since then! Excel XP doesn't just perform your own calculations quickly and accurately, it also offers, amongst other things:

- a full range of functions and wizards for analysing data;

- database-style sorting and searching facilities;

- full control over the layout and appearance of text and numbers;

- easy-to-use but sophisticated graphing routines that can make underlying trends and patterns more visible.

The sheet that calculates the bills can also produce professional-looking invoices, record the sales and update the inventory.

Two layers

With a word-processed document, what you see is what you get. Spreadsheets are different. The data that you enter the sheet is not necessarily what you see on the screen or printed output. You (normally) see the the results of calculations, not the formulae; numbers can be displayed in different formats (see page 57); text may appear cropped short if it is too long to fit; and confidential data or calculations can be hidden if desired.

Entering and editing data

Entering data into a spreadsheet is significantly different from entering it into a word processor. Data is entered and edited through the Formula line, which is linked to the current cell. It displays whatever is in the cell at the moment, and anything typed into the Formula line is transferred to the cell after editing.

1 Point at the target cell and click on it to make it current.

❑ To enter data

2 Start to type – if you are entering a formula start with an = sign.

❑ To edit cell contents

3 Click in the Formula line, or press [F2] to start editing.

4 Use the [←] / [→] keys to move along the Formula line; [Back-space] or [Delete] to erase errors.

5 Click   beside the Formula line, or press [Enter] when you have done. The data will appear in the cell.

Jargon

Current cell – the last one you clicked with the mouse. It is marked by a heavy border.

Cell reference – a Column letter/Row number combination that identifies a cell. Here the current cell is C3 (Column C, Row 3).

Range – a set of cells, which may be one or more full rows or columns, or a block somewhere in the middle of the sheet.

Formula line – the slot at the top. Its contents are transferred to the current cell when you press [Enter]. All data is entered into cells through this line.

Workbook – a set of sheets saved and used as one file. A formula in one sheet can draw in the data in any of the others.

Wide text will flow into empty cells

Column letters

Formula line

Fonts and Formats

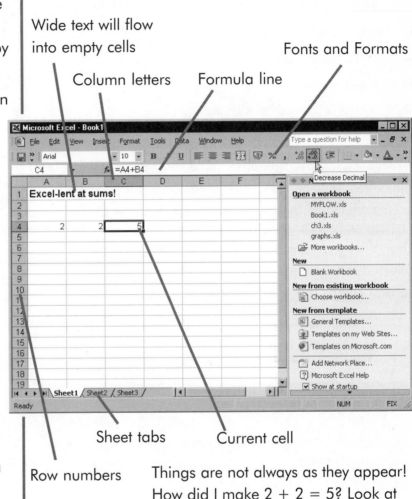

Sheet tabs

Current cell

Row numbers

Things are not always as they appear! How did I make 2 + 2 = 5? Look at the Formatting toolbar for a clue.

Take note

An Excel sheet has 256 columns and 65,536 rows — that's a total of 16,777,216 cells! And if this isn't enough, you can have as many sheets as you like in one workbook.

Selecting cells

Once you have selected a cell, or a range of cells, you can:

- apply a font style or alignment;
- add a border to some or all of its edges;
- erase its contents;
- use its references in a formula;
- move it to another position.

A range reference is made up of the cell references of the top left and bottom right corners. Most of the time you will be able to get the references by selecting the range with the mouse.

Shows the size of a block while it is being selected; otherwise the reference of the current cell or of the top left cell of a block

❑ To select a block

1 Point to the top left cell (or any corner).

2 Hold down the mouse button and drag the highlight over the block.

❑ To select a set of rows

3 Point to the row number at the top or bottom of the set.

4 Drag up or down over the numbers to high-light the rows you want.

1 Start here

2 Drag to the opposite corner

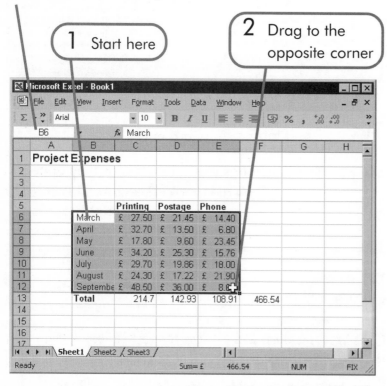

	A	B	C	D	E	F	G	H
1	Project Expenses							
2								
3								
4								
5			Printing	Postage	Phone			
6		March	£ 27.50	£ 21.45	£ 14.40			
7		April	£ 32.70	£ 13.50	£ 6.80			
8		May	£ 17.80	£ 9.60	£ 23.45			
9		June	£ 34.20	£ 25.30	£ 15.76			
10		July	£ 29.70	£ 19.86	£ 18.00			
11		August	£ 24.30	£ 17.22	£ 21.90			
12		Septembe	£ 48.50	£ 36.00	£ 8.8			
13		Total	214.7	142.93	108.91	466.54		
14								
15								
16								
17								

Microsoft Excel - Book1

File Edit View Insert Format Tools Data Window Help

Arial 10 B I U

B6 £ March

Sheet1 Sheet2 Sheet3

Ready Sum= £ 466.54 NUM FIX

Tip

In a selected range, all the cells will be shown in reverse colour, except for the first — the current cell. It's easy to think that this hasn't been selected. Don't be misled.

- ❏ To select a set of columns
- **5** Point to the letter of the first column.
- **6** Drag across the top of the columns to include the ones you want.
- ❏ To select all cells
- **7** Click in the top left corner, where the row and column headers meet.
- ❏ To select scattered cells
- **8** Select one, then hold down [Ctrl] key and click on the rest.

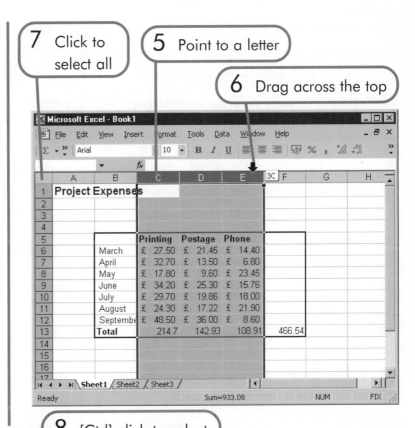

> **7** Click to select all

> **5** Point to a letter

> **6** Drag across the top

> **8** [Ctrl]-click to select

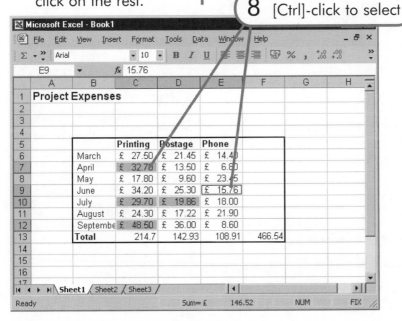

Take note

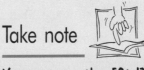

You can use the [Ctrl]-click technique to select cells for formatting or for use in a function, but a set of scattered cells cannot copied or moved.

Fonts and formats

Setting font types, styles and sizes for text is exactly the same here as it is in Word. Just select the cells and click a toolbar button or use **Format > Cells** and switch to the **Font** tab.

Number formats are a different matter. The way in which we write a number depends upon what it represents. If it is a money value, we would write a £ (or other currency sign) before and show two figures after the decimal point; with a large number, we would put commas every three digits to make it easier to read; if it is a percent, we place a % sign after it.

Excel knows about all this. It can display numbers in different formats, and can understand numbers that are written in different formats. Type in £12,345.67 and it will realise that the underlying number is 12345.67, and also that you want to display it as currency. Type in 50% and it will store it as 0.5, while showing 50% on screen. Type in 0181-123 4567 and it will not be fooled into thinking it's a sum – this gets treated as text. Try it and see for yourself.

Basic steps

1 Select the range of cells to be formatted.

2 From the Format menu select Cells...

3 On the Number tab, select a format from the Category list.

4 Set the number of decimal places.

5 With the *Number* and *Currency* formats, set the Negative numbers style.

6 With *Currency*, pick a Symbol if necessary.

7 Click [OK].

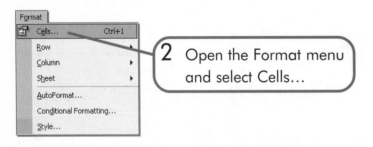

2 Open the Format menu and select Cells...

Take note

The Currency, Comma and Percent formats can be set from the Formatting toolbar buttons.

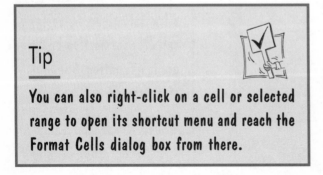

Tip

You can also right-click on a cell or selected range to open its shortcut menu and reach the Format Cells dialog box from there.

General displays most values in *Number* format, large ones in *Exponential*.

Number as [,], with commas every 3 digits, and 2 decimal places.

Currency as Number, with a currency sign (e.g. £) at the front.

Percent [%] multiplies the value by 100 and adds % at the end.

Fractions to nearest common fraction or up to 3 digit accuracy.

Scientific for very large or small numbers.

Text treats digits as text.

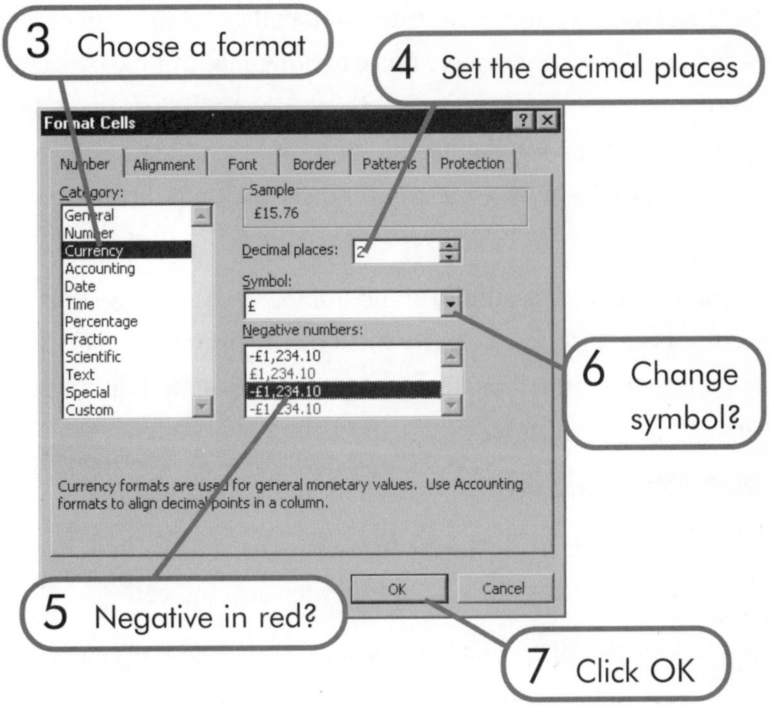

A small selection of the number formats that Excel can handle. The number of decimal places can be set in any format. With Currency and Number formats, you can have negative numbers shown in red.

If you see "######" increase the column width to display the number properly – you can pause over the cell to see the value in a pop-up

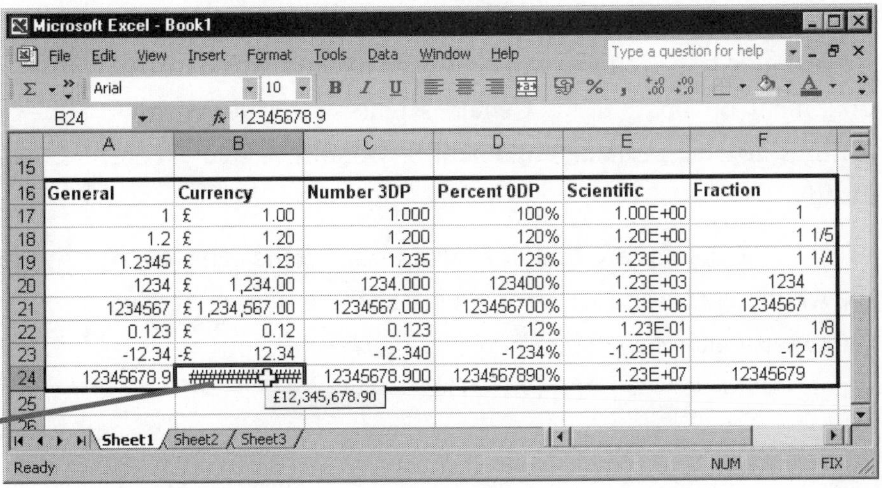

	A	B	C	D	E	F
16	General	Currency	Number 3DP	Percent 0DP	Scientific	Fraction
17	1	£ 1.00	1.000	100%	1.00E+00	1
18	1.2	£ 1.20	1.200	120%	1.20E+00	1 1/5
19	1.2345	£ 1.23	1.235	123%	1.23E+00	1 1/4
20	1234	£ 1,234.00	1234.000	123400%	1.23E+03	1234
21	1234567	£ 1,234,567.00	1234567.000	123456700%	1.23E+06	1234567
22	0.123	£ 0.12	0.123	12%	1.23E-01	1/8
23	-12.34	-£ 12.34	-12.340	-1234%	-1.23E+01	-12 1/3
24	12345678.9	###########	12345678.900	1234567890%	1.23E+07	12345679

Alignment

In Excel, all text must be written into cells, and this can create some problems. If you have more text than will fit into the cell, it will be cut short if there is something in the cell to its right. The simple solution – widening the column – can create its own problems as the extra wide column may mess up the display in the rows below or above.

A spreadsheet is essentially about numbers, so ensuring that the numbers are displayed clearly must be the prime aim. Any text should then be fitted as neatly as possible around that number display. Excel offers a number of solutions:

- **Wrap text**: text runs on two or more lines within the cell.

- **Shrink to fit**: text is reduced in size until it fits – handy for squeezing the odd extra letter into the cell.

- **Merge cells**: joins two or more cells together, allowing text in the leftmost to flow right across.

- **Orientation**: allows text to be displayed on the slant so that it takes up less width.

- **Merge and Center**: (on the Formatting toolbar) centres the text in the leftmost cell across a set of cells.

These are all available on the **Alignment** tab of the **Format Cells** dialog box. You will also find there the normal horizontal alignment options – Left, Center, Right and Justify – plus settings for the *vertical* alignment – Bottom, Center, Top, Justify.

Most of the options are straightforward – select the cells, go to the Alignment tab and set the options. The basic steps just cover the two trickier ones.

❑ Setting Orientation

1 Select the cells.

2 From the Format menu select Cells...

3 Switch to the Alignment tab.

4 Drag the red marker around the arc to set the angle.

5 Click ⬚ OK ⬚.

❑ Merge and center

6 Type the text into the leftmost cell of the set.

7 Select the set of cells.

8 Click ⊞.

> **Take note**
>
> By default, numbers are aligned to the right, text to the left.

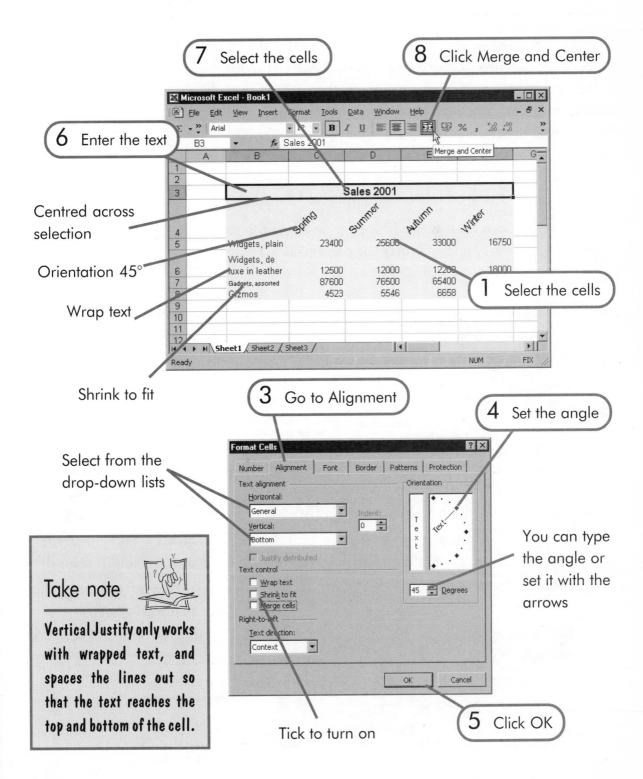

7 Select the cells

8 Click Merge and Center

6 Enter the text

Centred across
selection

Orientation 45°

Wrap text

Shrink to fit

1 Select the cells

3 Go to Alignment

4 Set the angle

Select from the
drop-down lists

You can type
the angle or
set it with the
arrows

Take note

Vertical Justify only works
with wrapped text, and
spaces the lines out so
that the text reaches the
top and bottom of the cell.

Tick to turn on

5 Click OK

59

Autoformats

Excel's Autoformats, like Word's, offer an instant design solution for common situations. They are all based on headed tables or lists, but with 17 alternatives to choose from, you should find something there to suit most of your needs. The formatting includes that of the numbers, the style of text and the size of the rows and columns as well as shading and borders. If you have some formatting already in place, e.g. the number display, you can choose not to overwrite it with the AutoFormat.

Colours and shades are best avoided if you are not using a colour printer, as they will be printed in grey and could be darker than you expect – making text difficult to read.

Basic steps

1 Select the table or list to be formatted, including its headers and totals.

2 Open the Format menu and select AutoFormat...

3 Scroll through and pick a format.

4 If there are aspects you do not want to apply, click Options... and clear the checkbox by those options.

5 Click OK.

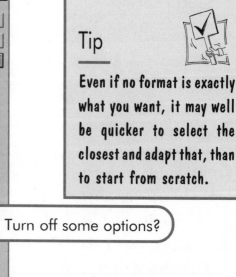

2 Use Format > AutoFormat...

3 Select a format

5 Click OK

4 Turn off some options?

Tip

Even if no format is exactly what you want, it may well be quicker to select the closest and adapt that, than to start from scratch.

Basic steps

❏ To total a range

1 Click on the cell below the column (or to the right of the row).

2 Click the Σ⋅ Autosum button.

3 You will see that the column (or row) is highlighted, and that there is =SUM(*range*) in the formula line.

4 If the range covers the right cells, click or press [Enter] to accept the formula.

You won't get far with a spreadsheet without writing formulae, but at least Excel makes it a fairly painless business. If you just want to total a column or row of figures, it only takes a click of a button with **Autosum**. Other calculations take a little more effort, but point and click references, and readily-accessible lists of functions simplify the process and reduce the chance of errors.

A formula starts with the = sign and can contain a mixture of cell or range references, numbers, text and functions, joined by operators. These include the arithmetic symbols / (divide) * (multiply) + (add) − (subtract) ^ (power) and a few others.

Examples of simple formulae:

= 4 * C1   4 times the contents of cell C1

= B3+B4   the value in B3 added to that in B4

=SUM(A5:A12)   the sum of the values in cells A5 to A12.

References can be typed into the formula line, or pulled in by clicking on a cell or highlighting a range.

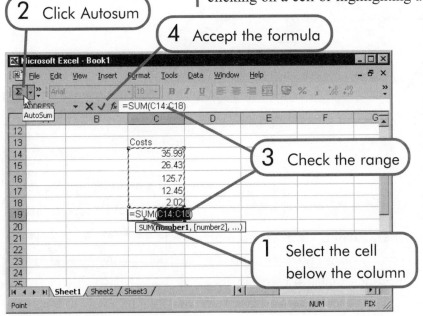

2 Click Autosum

4 Accept the formula

3 Check the range

1 Select the cell below the column

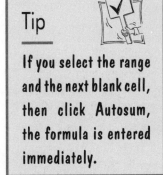

Tip

If you select the range and the next blank cell, then click Autosum, the formula is entered immediately.

Mathematical formulae

The following operators can be used in Excel formulae:

+	addition	–	subtraction
*	multiplication	/	division
^	raise to the power	()	brackets

Where there are several operators in a formula, the normal rules of precedence are followed: power, then multiplication/division, and finally addition/subtraction.

Operations in brackets are performed first; e.g. $4 * 3 + 2 = 14$, but $4 * (3 + 2) = 20$.

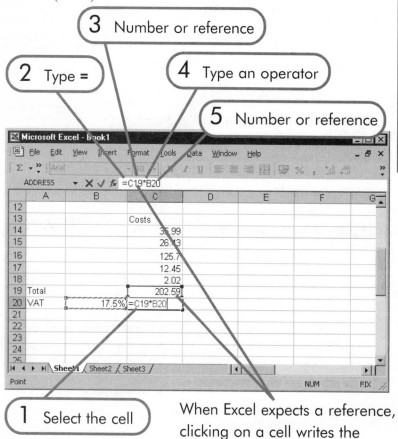

3 Number or reference

2 Type =

4 Type an operator

5 Number or reference

1 Select the cell

When Excel expects a reference, clicking on a cell writes the reference into the formula

Basic steps

- [ ] To write a formula

1 Click on the cell where the formula is to go.

2 Type '='.

3 Type the number, or point and click to get a cell reference.

4 Type an operator.

5 Type the next number, or select the next reference.

6 Repeat steps 4 and 5, as necessary, to complete the formula.

7 Click ☑ or press [Enter].

Tip

If a cell displays the formula, not its result, there is an error in it. Select the cell and press [F2] to edit it.

62

Using names

Basic steps

❑ To name a range

1 Select the cell or the range.

2 Open the Insert menu and select Name then Define…

3 An adjacent text item may be suggested as the name – edit it or type a new name.

4 Click [OK].

❑ To remove a name

5 Open the Define Name… dialog box.

6 Highlight the name and click [Delete].

Cell and range references are hard to remember, and if you reorganise the layout of the spreadsheet, you may have to learn them all again. To make life simpler, Excel allows you to give meaningful names to cells and ranges. Use them. They will make your formulae more readable, and if you want to transfer data into a word processed document, you can only do this with named ranges.

2 Use Insert > Name > Define

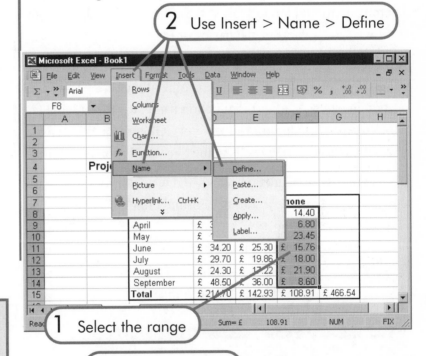

1 Select the range

3 Define the name

4 Click OK

6 Click Delete

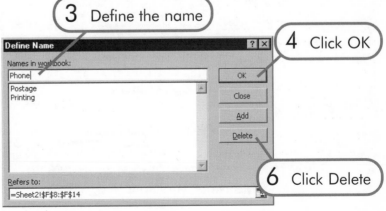

Take note

Deleting a name does not affect anything else. The contents of the cells will be untouched, and references will replace any names that were used in formulae.

Functions

A function takes one or more number or text values, performs some kind of process on them and gives a new value in return. It may be a simple process, as with SUM, which adds up a range of numbers. It may be a familiar one such as SIN, which gives the sine of an angle. It may be a complex process that you wouldn't meet anywhere except on a spreadsheet. PMT, for example, will give you the regular repayment on a mortgage. There is no room here to look at these functions properly, but what we can do is cover the basics of how to use them.

Almost all functions take one or more *arguments*. These can be values, cell or range references or other functions. They are written in brackets, after the function name, e.g. INT(3.141) – which converts a value to an integer – or COUNT(B1:B9,D1:D9) – which finds how many cells in the two ranges contain values.

If you know how a function works and what sort of arguments it needs, you can type it into the Formula line. In general, it is simpler to use the function list and the Paste Function dialog box, and be guided through the construction of the function.

1 Select the cell into which the formula should go.

2 Type '='.

3 Drop down the function list.

4 If you can see the one you want, select it.

Otherwise

5 Click More Functions…

6 Select a category, then a function and click OK.

7 To select a cell or range, click ⌐ to shrink the Function Arguments panel.

8 Select the cell/range to get the reference and click ▣ to reopen the panel.

9 Enter other references or values as required and click OK.

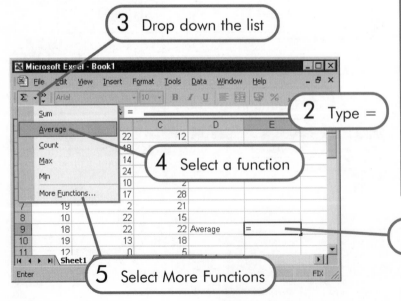

3 Drop down the list

2 Type =

4 Select a function

1 Select the cell

5 Select More Functions

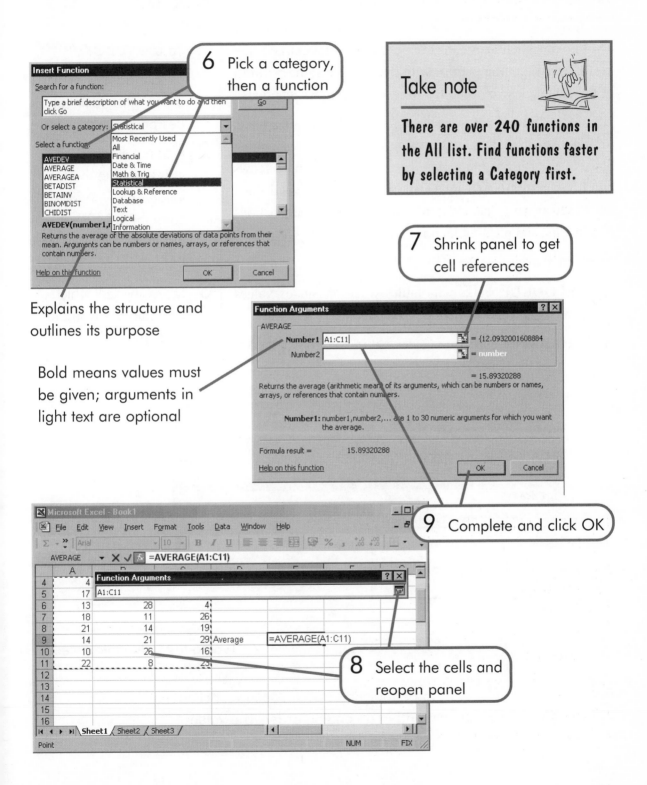

6 Pick a category, then a function

Explains the structure and outlines its purpose

Bold means values must be given; arguments in light text are optional

Take note

There are over 240 functions in the All list. Find functions faster by selecting a Category first.

7 Shrink panel to get cell references

9 Complete and click OK

8 Select the cells and reopen panel

Lookup functions

The Lookup functions are worth exploration – they can be really useful, and in getting to grips with these you will master most of the techniques you need for working with other functions.

A Lookup function will scan through a list of items in a table, to find a key item, then pick a value out of the corresponding place in another column within the table. The example shows two Lookup formulae being used on a simple price and stock list. When an item's name is typed into a key cell, the functions scan the list and pick out its price and stock level.

There are two similar functions.

- **HLOOKUP** works with tables where the index values are written across the top of the table;

- **VLOOKUP** expects the index values to be down the left side of the table.

❑ To use VLOOKUP

1 Create a table of data, with index values on the left.

2 Pick a cell into which you will write the key value and type in something which is in the table. This will test the formula.

3 Select the cell which will hold the formula and type '='.

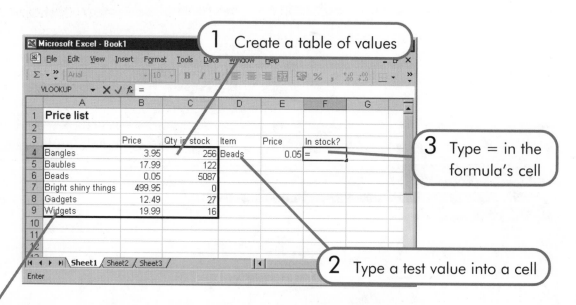

1 Create a table of values

3 Type = in the formula's cell

2 Type a test value into a cell

The index items – the ones to be matched by the Lookup function – must be in the first column and in ascending order. The values to be looked up are in columns to its right.

4 Drop down the function list and select More Functions…

5 Open the Lookup and Reference category, and select VLOOKUP.

6 For the *Lookup_value*, select or enter the reference of the cell containing your key value.

7 Click into *Table_array* and select the range that covers the table.

8 For *Col_index_num*, type 2 to get values from the first column to the right of the index values, or 3 to get values from the second column.

9 Click [OK].

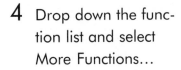

Take note

Recently used functions are added to the drop-down list.

5 Select VLOOKUP

6 Give the key cell

7 Select the table reference

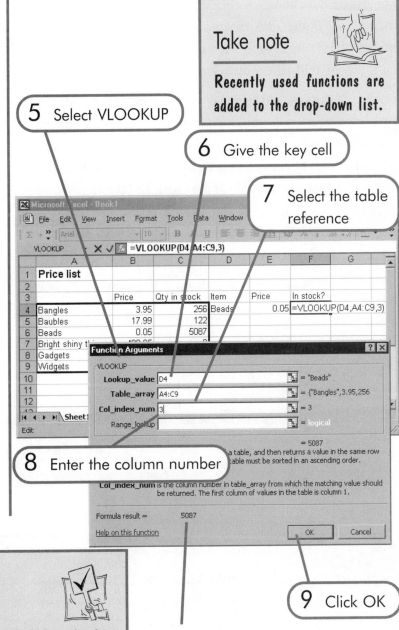

8 Enter the column number

9 Click OK

Tip

If the cell displays ERR, check that the key value really is in the table, then check the range reference. Those are the most likely errors.

If the Formula result is not what you expect, check the references

Charts

You can produce some lovely charts with Excel – and with very little effort. If the data that you want to chart is organised properly in the first place, then charting is a breeze – and if it isn't, the job will take a little longer, but is still not difficult.

Ideally, the data should be in a continuous block – no unwanted rows or columns in the middle – with headings above and to the side. If the data is in rows, i.e. each row is displayed as a line on a graph or a set of bars on a chart, then the top headings will be used to label the bottom axis of the chart, and the side headings will identify the rows in the legend. Where the data is in columns, the headings will be used the other way round.

With data in this form, you can simply run the Chart Wizard, which will collect a few choices from you and create the graph.

Basic steps

1 Select the data to be charted, along with the relevant headers.

2 Click ⬛ the Chart Wizard tool.

3 Select a Chart Type, then a sub-type, or a Custom Type and click [Next >].

4 Check the Data range – click ⌐ if you need to redefine the range – and the Series in Rows/Columns setting. Click [Next >].

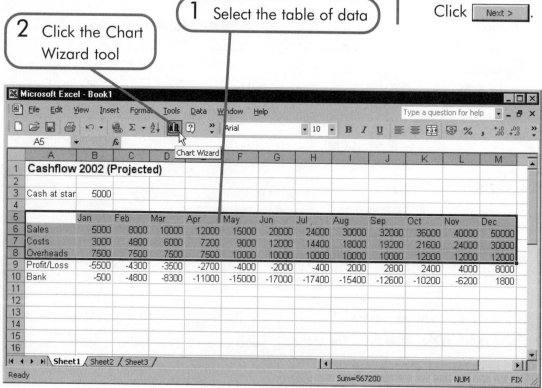

1 Select the table of data

2 Click the Chart Wizard tool

5 Enter the Chart title and Axis labels, if wanted.

6 Explore the options on the other tabs.

cont...

3 Select the type and sub-type

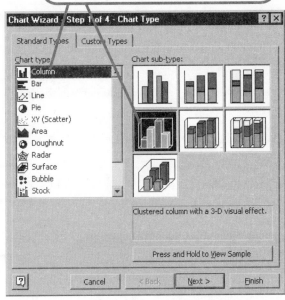

There are 14 types and 70 sub-types and 20 custom types to choose from!

6 Set other options

These all control the display of items around the main chart

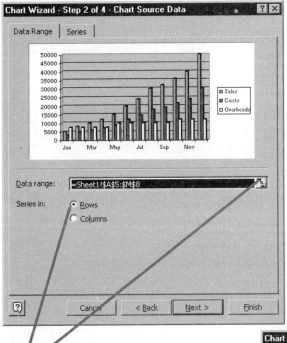

4 Set the range and Series in value

5 Enter the titles

Titles are not necessary on the axes if their meaning is obvious – e.g. 'time' or 'value'

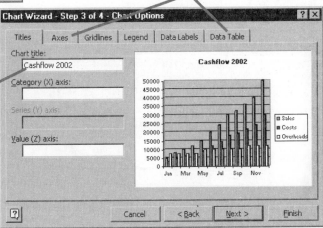

cont...

7 Where do you want it?

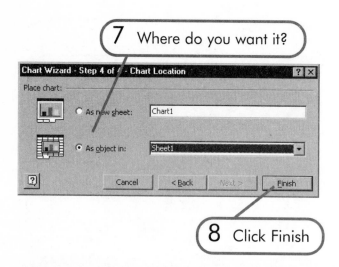

7 Select where the chart is to go – as a new sheet or as an object in an existing sheet.

8 Click [Finish].

9 If the chart is placed in a sheet, the Wizard will drop it into the middle – drag it into place and resize it.

8 Click Finish

9 Move and resize as needed

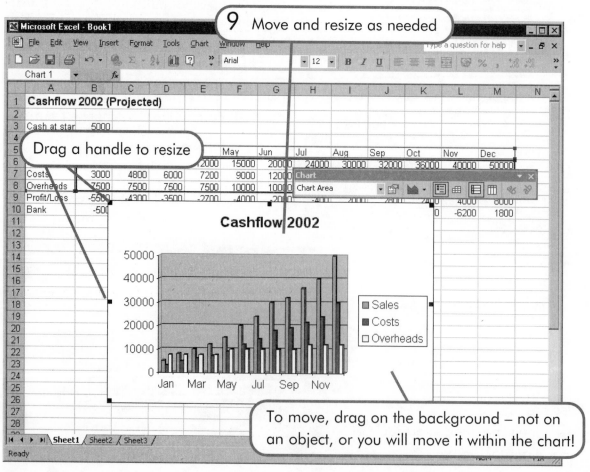

Drag a handle to resize

To move, drag on the background – not on an object, or you will move it within the chart!

Formatting charts

1 Right-click on a bar in the series.

2 Select Chart Type... and set it to Line – only that series will be affected.

3 Right-click on the line and select a Format Data Series...

4 To plot the line series against the right-hand axis, go to the Axis tab and select Secondary axis.

Using two axes lets you compare different ranges of values

Almost every aspect of a chart can be formatted individually to give you just the effect you want – right-click on any object to see the options on its short menu. Fonts, colours, line styles and similar are formatted as elsewhere in Office. A few options are unique to graphs. Here, for example is how to display one series as a line within a bar chart, with its own axis.

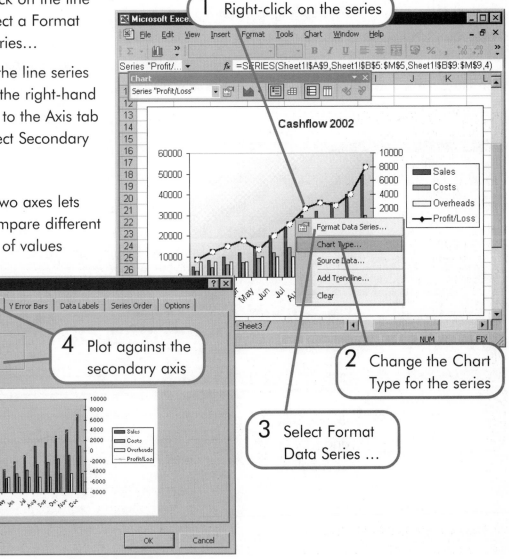

71

Printing

Printing is not as straightforward in Excel as in some applications. Spreadsheets are of indefinite size and highly variable layout, so the printout may fit on a single page or be spread across many. To get a good-looking printout you may have to adjust the orientation of the paper, the scale of the print and other aspects.

If the sheet will need more than one page, use the **Page Setup** panel to define how it will be split up for printing and to add headers/footers and other optional extras. Use the Print Preview to check that your setup works, before you commit it to paper.

Normally, the whole active area, i.e. where the cells contain data, will be printed.

Basic steps

1 Select the cells if you only want to print part of the active sheet.

2 From the File menu select Page Setup....

3 On the Page tab, set the Orientation and Scaling – reduce large sheets or set the Fit to pages options.

4 On the Sheet tab, define the Print area if needed, and set the Rows and Columns to repeat for labels on multi-page printing.

Page Setup `? X`

Page | Margins | Header/Footer | Sheet

Orientation
- ○ Portrait
- ● Landscape

Print...
Print Preview
Options...

Scaling
- ○ Adjust to: 100 % normal size
- ● Fit to: 2 page(s) wide by 3 tall

Paper size: A4 (210 x 297 mm)
Print quality: High
First page number: Auto

OK

3 Set Orientation and Scaling

Repeat Rows and Columns as labels?

4 Define the Print area?

5 Click Print Preview

Page Setup

Page | Margins | Header/Footer | Sheet

Print area: $A$1:$N$31
Print titles
Rows to repeat at top: $1:$1
Columns to repeat at left:

Print
- ☑ Gridlines
- ☐ Black and white
- ☐ Draft quality
- ☐ Row and column headings
- Comments: (None)
- Cell errors as: displayed

Page order
- ● Down, then over
- ○ Over, then down

Print...
Print Preview
Options...

OK   Cancel

Which way will the pages flow together best?

5 Click  Print Preview.

6 Check the preview. If it needs adjusting, click Setup... to return to the Page Setup.

7 Click Print... .

8 Set the Print range, Number of copies and other options as usual.

9 Click OK .

Take note

If it is a small sheet, or you have already defined your print options and want to use the same settings, just click 🖨.

Check the Fit to page and Page order settings before entering the Print range

7 Click Print

6 Click Setup to adjust

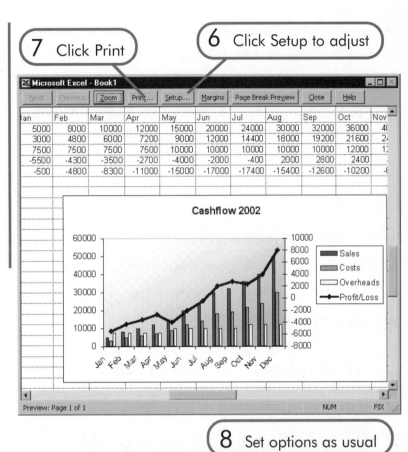

Microsoft Excel - Book1

Next | Previous | Zoom | Print... | Setup... | Margins | Page Break Preview | Close | Help

Jan	Feb	Mar	Apr	May	Jun	Jul	Aug	Sep	Oct	Nov
5000	8000	10000	12000	15000	20000	24000	30000	32000	36000	40
3000	4800	6000	7200	9000	12000	14400	18000	19200	21600	2
7500	7500	7500	7500	10000	10000	10000	10000	10000	12000	1
-5500	-4300	-3500	-2700	-4000	-2000	-400	2000	2800	2400	
-500	-4800	-8300	-11000	-15000	-17000	-17400	-15400	-12600	-10200	-

Cashflow 2002

Sales
Costs
Overheads
Profit/Loss

Preview: Page 1 of 1   NUM   FIX

8 Set options as usual

9 Click OK

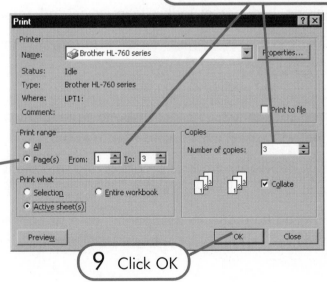

Print

Printer
Name: Brother HL-760 series   Properties...
Status: Idle
Type: Brother HL-760 series
Where: LPT1:
Comment: Print to file

Print range
○ All
● Page(s) From: 1 To: 3

Print what
○ Selection   ○ Entire workbook
● Active sheet(s)

Copies
Number of copies: 3

☑ Collate

Preview   OK   Close

Summary

❏ An Excel sheet is a grid of cells, each identified by its row and column reference.

❏ A cell's contents and its screen display may differ.

❏ Rows and columns can be selected by their header numbers and letters; blocks are selected by dragging from one corner to the opposite one.

❏ The appearance of the sheet can be enhanced by the use of fonts, alignments, borders and shading.

❏ Numbers can be displayed in different formats.

❏ The alignment options give you many ways to fit text within and across cells.

❏ The Autoformat options provide a quick way to give a professional finish to tables.

❏ Formulae all start with = and may include a mixture of text and number values, cell and range reference and functions.

❏ If you are going to use cells and ranges in formulae, giving them names makes them easier to handle.

❏ There is a wide range of functions, organised into several categories. They are easily accessed through the Insert Function dialog box.

❏ The Lookup functions allow you to write formulae that will extract information from a table.

❏ You can easily produce attractive and informative charts from tables of data.

❏ Printing normally needs planning as a spreadsheet may well not fit neatly onto sheets of paper.

5 Powerpoint

Introducing PowerPoint

PowerPoint is used for producing presentations, to be viewed as overhead projections, directly on a computer, through a Web browser or even as a proper slide show.

A presentation may contain:

- **text**, typically in bullet points, though larger blocks of text can be written;

- **images** – clip art, scanned pictures, photographs and drawings – which may be essential illustrations or just to brighten things up;

- **video and sound clips**, and even recorded commentary synchronised with the presentations;

- **graphs, diagrams, organisation charts** and embedded objects from other applications.

All of these can be formatted in the usual ways, and displayed on a coloured, patterned or picture background.

The central part of any presentation is a set of 'slides'. At the simplest, these will be displayed, in full, one after the other, but if you want more, you can have animated transitions between slides, build slide displays by flying in their components one by one or using other visual effects, and let the audience pick its own path through the set.

Each slide can be accompanied by notes, which can be printed out for the presenter's benefit, or incorporated into handouts for the audience. The handouts can be anything from simple reminders, with the slides printed in miniature nine to a page, or full course notes – you can even use PowerPoint in the same way as you would use Word, to produce full pages of text and images.

Take note

This chapter gives a quick introduction to the essentials of PowerPoint. See Chapters 6 and 7 for more about working with text, images and other objects.

The PowerPoint window

This has three views.

- **Normal view** is best for general work. Open the **Outline tab** when you want to concentrate on the text and the **Slide tab** for adjusting the order of the slides.

- Use **Slide Sorter view** for a better overview of the show and for a simpler way to reorganise the order.

- Use **Slide Show view** to see the presentation in action.

Slide tab

Outline tab

Standard toolbar

Formatting toolbar

Slide pane

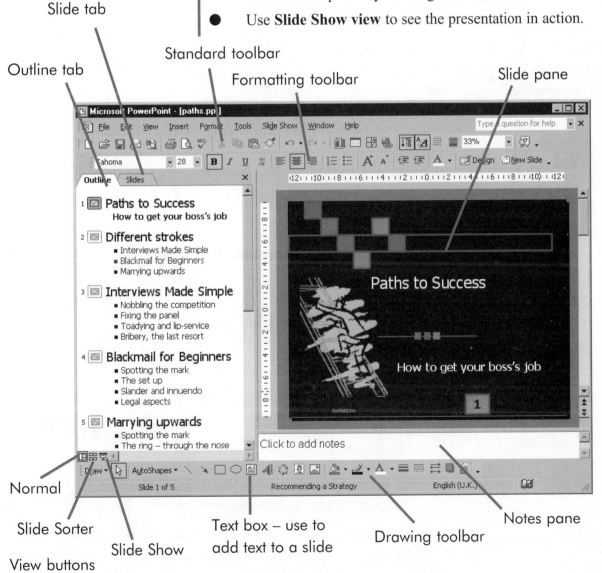

Normal

Slide Sorter

Slide Show

View buttons

Text box – use to add text to a slide

Drawing toolbar

Notes pane

New presentation

PowerPoint offers three approaches to creating a presentation.

- **Blank presentation** leaves it entirely up to you;

- **Design Templates** have the background and the font styles, sizes and colours set up for you;

- **AutoContent Wizard** and **Presentation Templates** have the design elements in place, plus whole structure of the presentation, with suggested content.

Here's how to start from a Design Template.

1 In the Task Pane, click Design Template. (If Task Pane is not open, used File > New to open it.)

2 Select a template by clicking on it. If you want to use the default layout, go to step 5.

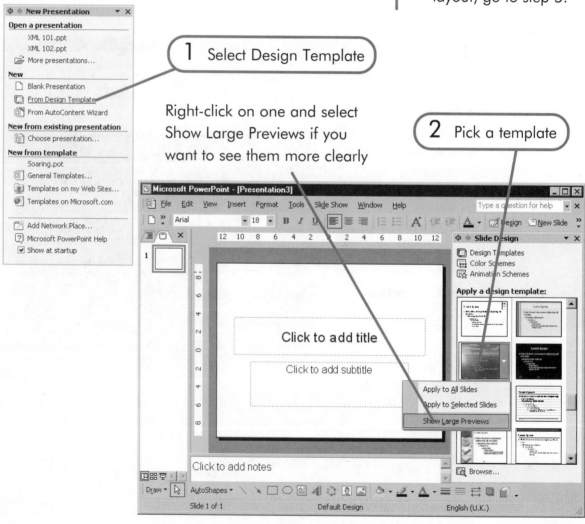

1 Select Design Template

Right-click on one and select Show Large Previews if you want to see them more clearly

2 Pick a template

3 To change to a different layout, open the Format menu and select Slide Layout to display the options in the Task Pane.

4 Click on the arrow bar of the layout you want and select Apply to Selected Slides.

5 Replace the *Click to add text* prompts with your own text – just click and type.

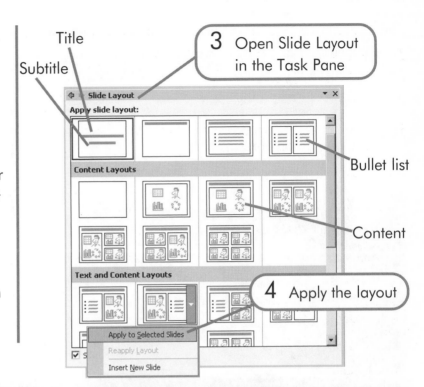

Title

Subtitle

3 Open Slide Layout in the Task Pane

Bullet list

Content

4 Apply the layout

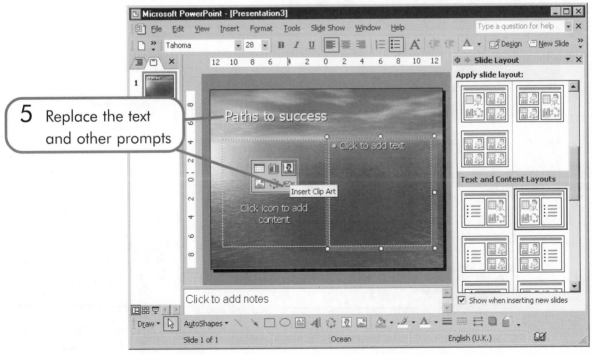

5 Replace the text and other prompts

Off-the-shelf presentations

There are 24 of these, which you can reach either through the Presentations tab of the New Presentation dialog box or the AutoContent Wizard – the Wizard simply collects a little information before opening.

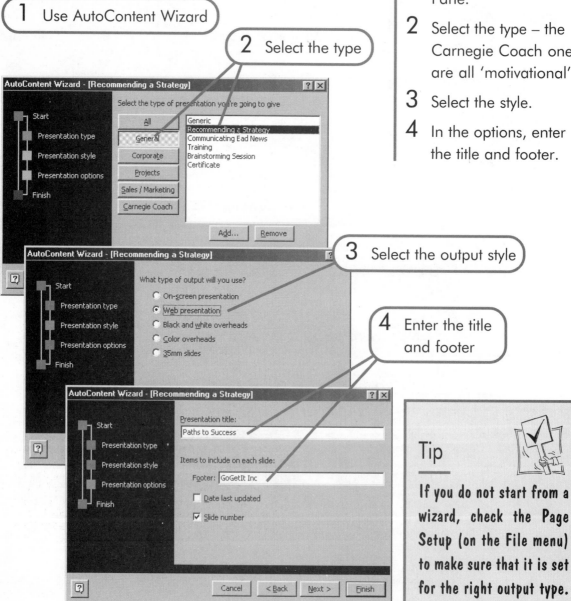

❑ Using the Wizard

1 Select AutoContent Wizard from the New Presentation Task Pane.

2 Select the type – the Carnegie Coach ones are all 'motivational'.

3 Select the style.

4 In the options, enter the title and footer.

Tip

If you do not start from a wizard, check the Page Setup (on the File menu) to make sure that it is set for the right output type.

- ❑ The Presentations tab

5 Select General Templates... from the New Presentation Task Pane.

6 Open the Presentations tab of the Templates dialog box.

7 Select a presentation and click [OK].

8 With the Outline tab on top, replace the titles and other text.

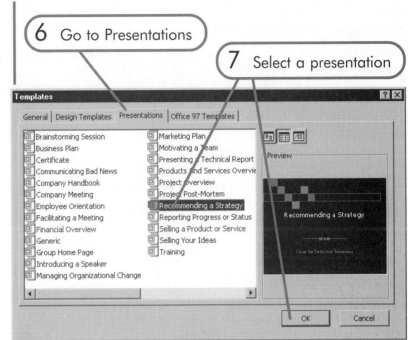

Editing text is simplest in Outline tab

Text on slides

Once you have got text onto a slide, it can be edited and formatted in the same way as text in Word – the difference is in how you get the text there. You cannot simply type onto a slide.

- If the slide layout has title and text boxes, you can click and replace their prompts.

- If you want to add a title to a blank slide, you can type it into the Outline tab, after the slide's icon.

- To add any other text to a slide, you must insert a text box and type into there. Don't worry too much about placing it accurately – it can be moved or resized freely, so you can get your text exactly where and how you want it.

Basic steps

1 Open the Insert menu and select Text box.

Or

2 Click 🔳 on the Drawing toolbar.

3 Click where you want one corner of the box and drag an outline.

4 Type your text, then format it as normal.

5 Drag the outline to move, or a handle to resize the text box.

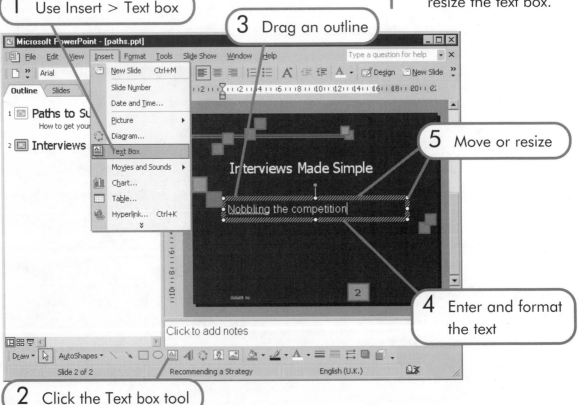

1 Use Insert > Text box

3 Drag an outline

5 Move or resize

4 Enter and format the text

2 Click the Text box tool

82

Basic steps

1 Open the Insert menu and select New Slide.

2 Select a Layout containing one or more content boxes.

3 Click on the icon for desired content.

4 What happens next varies, but expect to be prompted to add your text or other data. You can usually add components to build more complex diagrams.

Tip

If you want to change the layout of an existing slide, use Format > Slide Layout and select a new layout.

Content boxes

If you want pictures, charts or other objects on a slide, start from a slide containing a Content box. Click on the required icon to start its insert routine.

Table – see page 124

Chart – see the next page and page 128

Clip Art – see page 112

Picture – see page 112

Diagram or Organization Chart – see page 120

Media clip – see page 114

1 Use Insert > New Slide

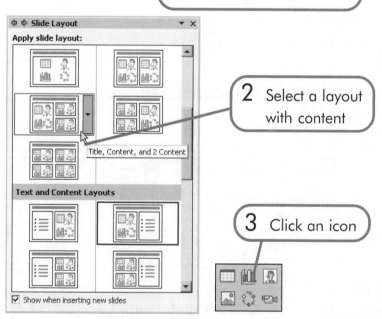

2 Select a layout with content

Title, Content, and 2 Content

3 Click an icon

Tip

To add an object to an existing slide, use options on the Insert menu.

Charts

If you want a chart in a slide (or any document), there are two main ways to do it: insert a chart from an Excel worksheet (see Chapter 8) or use Microsoft Graph to create one on the slide.

The basic chart is ready-made for you, with dummy data in its linked datasheet. At the simplest, all you need to do is replace the dummy data, adding more rows or columns if required.

● Start from a slide with a content box, clicking its Chart icon, or from one with a chart icon.

Basic steps

1 On a slide with a content or chart box, click the chart icon.

2 Replace the dummy data, adding more if needed.

3 Close the datasheet to see the chart clearly.

❑ For guidance on formatting charts, see pages 68–71 and 128–129.

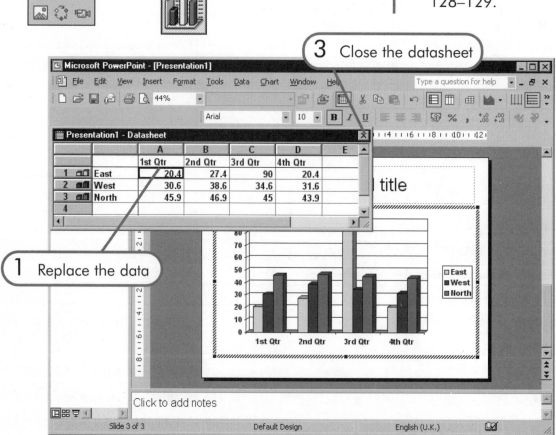

Basic steps

1 Switch to Slide Sorter view.

2 Click on the slide to be moved and hold down the button.

3 Drag across the screen – a line will show where the slide will be placed.

4 Release the mouse button.

Slide Sorter view

The main purpose of this view is – of course – for sorting slides, but it can also be useful to give you an overview of the whole set. Are they all too much the same? With shorter presentations, consistency can be a good thing, but too much of the same is something else! Are the illustrations, if any, spaced to (re)capture your audience's attention? You can, and should, test your presentation to check just these things, but at an early stage, Slide Sorter view gives you a quick way to see it all.

Reorganising the order of slides is simple.

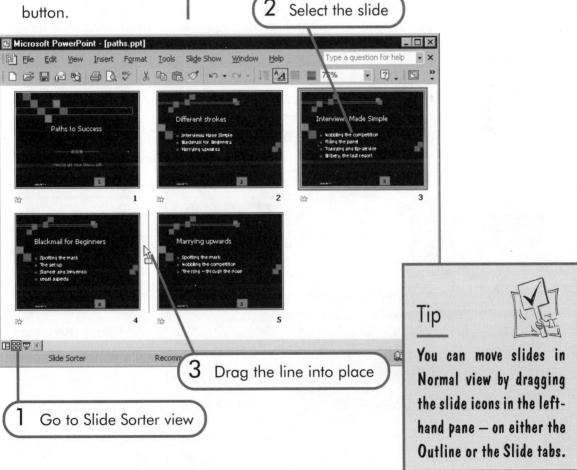

2 Select the slide

3 Drag the line into place

1 Go to Slide Sorter view

Tip

You can move slides in Normal view by dragging the slide icons in the left-hand pane – on either the Outline or the Slide tabs.

Transition and Animation

Slide transition controls how the show progresses from one slide to another. You can specify:

- How a slide becomes visible – selecting from a wide range of uncovering, dissolves, blinds and other effects.

- The speed of the transition.

- Accompanying sound effects – go easy on these, they can put the audience off if overdone.

- When the new slide should appear – after a set time or on a mouse click.

If none are set, then the presenter will have to run the show manually, using the keyboard or mouse, and slides will simply come on screen, replacing the previous one.

When you select an effect, you'll see a preview of it

Basic steps

1 Open the Slide Show menu and select Slide Transition...

2 Select an Effect.

3 Set the speed.

4 Pick a Sound if useful.

5 Turn on Automatically after and set the timing, if wanted.

6 The transition will be applied to that slide – click [Apply to All Slides] to apply it to them all.

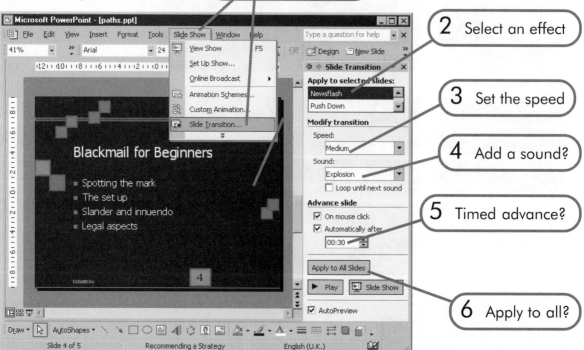

1 Use Slide Show > Slide Transition

2 Select an effect

3 Set the speed

4 Add a sound?

5 Timed advance?

6 Apply to all?

Basic steps

1 Open the Slide Show menu and select Animation Schemes...

2 Select a scheme – it will be previewed on the current slide.

3 Click [Apply to All Slides] if you want to apply it to all the slides.

Animations can be set in either Normal or Slide Sorter view

Animation

This controls how the elements of a slide are brought into view. At the simplest, they are all in place when the slide is first displayed. At the most complex, you can specify a different animation for each element of every slide. In between, there are a range of preset animations that you can apply with a single style to the whole set – here's how.

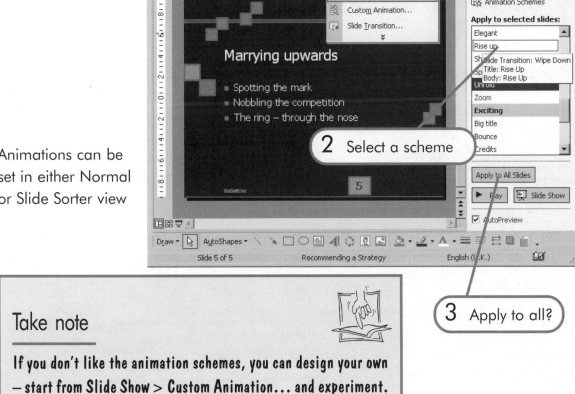

2 Use Slide Show > Animation Schemes

2 Select a scheme

3 Apply to all?

Take note

If you don't like the animation schemes, you can design your own – start from Slide Show > Custom Animation... and experiment.

Running a presentation

To run a slide show, you can simply click the Slide Show view button to start it, then click the left mouse button to bring up each slide. However, if you spend a few minutes beforehand you can ensure that it runs just how you want it, and if you make a little effort during the presentation, you can get more out of it.

In the Set Up Show dialog box, the main settings are the Show type and the Advance slides. If you want a self-running demonstration, use the Browsed at a kiosk option, and timed advance.

1 Open the Slide Show menu and select Set Up Show...

2 Set the Show type.

3 For a partial show, set the From: and To: values.

4 Turn on the Show without ... options for a quicker show.

5 Set the Advance slides option.

6 Choose a pen colour if you'll be using it.

7 Click [OK].

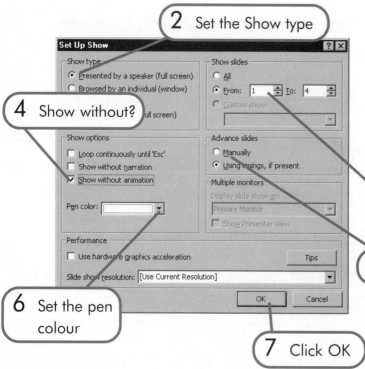

2 Set the Show type

4 Show without?

3 Which slides?

5 Manual or timed?

6 Set the pen colour

7 Click OK

Rehearsing timings

Use this routine to check that your presentation will fit into the time allowed, and to see where you can expand or make cuts if necessary. When you run it, a timer/control panel is present as you talk through your show. At the end, you will see the total time; the time on each slide can be shown in Slide Sorter view.

Timings control panel

Time for current slide

Total time so far

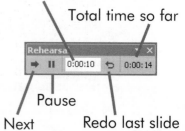

Pause

Next

Redo last slide

Interactive presentations

The right-click menu that you can call up during a presentation, contains some useful tools.

- **Next**, **Previous**, the **Go** menu and **End Show** allow you to navigate freely through the show.

- The **Meeting Minder** lets you make notes and 'Action Items' as you go. These can all be called up from the **Tools** menu afterwards for reference, and – even better – the Action Items are automatically collated and displayed on a new slide at the end of the presentation.

- **Speaker Notes** displays any notes you added to a slide, in case you lose your way and your printed notes!

- **Screen** lets you black out the display temporarily.

- **Pointer Options** allow you to hide the pointer, or switch to a pen so that you can draw on the screen to emphasise a point.

The Pen Color should be selected in the Set Up Show dialog box to avoid delays during the show

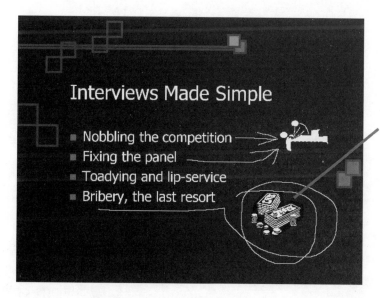

There's a real art to drawing smoothly on screen with a mouse – and very few of us ever acquire it!

Printing

As PowerPoint is based on slides, there is little room for variation in printing. The main choices are which parts of the presentation to print, which slides to include and how many copies. There is no Print Preview, such as in Word, as the output is the same on screen and paper, but there are two other previews.

● If the slides are for viewing by a browser, **Web Page Preview** will open your browser and display them.

● The Grayscale or Pure Black and White views may be worth checking before output to a black-only printer. If you have images that do not come out well in the default black and white or grayscale, you can adjust the shading through the Settings options on the Grayscale View toolbar.

Use View > Grayscale or Black and White for the preview

If you need to adjust the shading of an image, try a different Settings option

Basic steps

❏ Instant print

1 Click 🖶.

❏ Controlled printing

2 Open the File menu and select Print.

3 Select a different Printer if required.

4 Set the range of pages or slides to print.

5 Set the number of copies.

6 Select a Print What option – *Slides, Hand-outs, Notes Pages* or *Outline view.*

7 For Handouts, set the number per page.

8 Set the other options as required.

9 Click [OK].

For a straight printout of all the slides (or to use the same settings as the last time you did a controlled print), just click the Print button. For anything else, use the menu command.

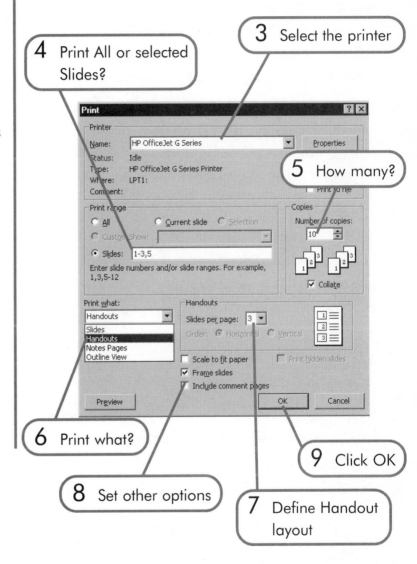

4 Print All or selected Slides?

3 Select the printer

5 How many?

6 Print what?

8 Set other options

9 Click OK

7 Define Handout layout

Summary

❑ A PowerPoint presentation can combine text with images, sound and video clips and objects from other applications.

❑ Use Blank Document to start a new presentation from scratch; a Design Template to start with a style colour and font scheme; AutoContent Wizard or the Presentation Templates for a ready-made structure.

❑ To enter text onto a slide, you must replace an existing prompt or create a text box.

❑ Pictures, diagrams and other objects can be added through Content placeholders, or inserted at will.

❑ Use Slide Sorter view to rearrange the order of slides.

❑ You can set transitions to enliven the change from one slide to the next.

❑ There are animations that you can use to build a display one element at a time.

❑ Presentations can be set up to be run by a presenter or a viewer, or to be self-running.

❑ When printing in black and white, you can preview the output and adjust the shading of images if necessary.

❑ You can choose which part of the presentation and which slides to print.

6 Working with text

Selecting text

There are essentially two approaches to formatting text.

- You can set the style, type the text, then turn the style off, or set a new style.

- Or you can type in your text, then go back over it, selecting blocks and formatting them.

It is generally simplest to type the text first and format it to suit later – but before you can format it, you must select it.

These selection techniques apply to text in Excel cells and Powerpoint elements, and anywhere in Word documents.

□ With a mouse

1 Point to the start of the text to be selected.

2 Hold down the left button, drag to the end and release the button.

□ With the [Shift] key

3 Move the I-beam to the first character.

4 Hold down [Shift] and use the arrow keys to move to the end, then release [Shift].

Tip

You can select a word by double-clicking in it or a paragraph by triple-clicking in it.

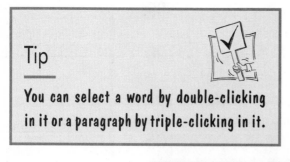

1 Point to the start

3 Move to the start

Selecting text

There are essentially two approaches to formatting text.

- You can set the style, **type the text**, then turn the style off, *or set a new style*.

- Or you can type in your text, then go back over it, selecting blocks and formatting them.

It is generally simplest to type the text first and format it to suit later – but before you can format it, you must select it.

4 [Shift] and move to the end

2 Drag to the end

Select whole columns by
selecting their letters

Click here to select
the whole sheet

Select whole rows
by selecting their
numbers

You can select
and format a
block in a cell

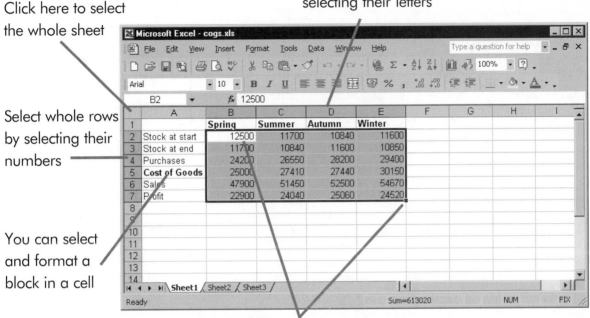

Select a block by dragging from
one corner to the opposite corner

To select one or
more elements,
drag an outline
to enclose them

Blocks within
the text can be
selected in the
usual ways

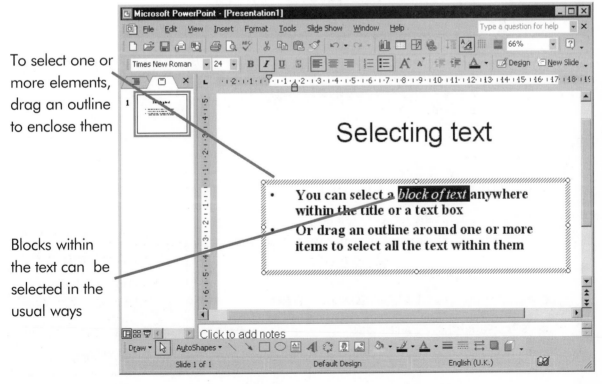

Fonts

The Formatting Toolbars

These hold all the tools you need for everyday work. There are minor differences between the applications, reflecting their different requirements.

Basic steps

1 Select the text.

2 Click the Toolbar buttons to set fonts and styles.

or

3 Right-click within the selected area to open the short menu.

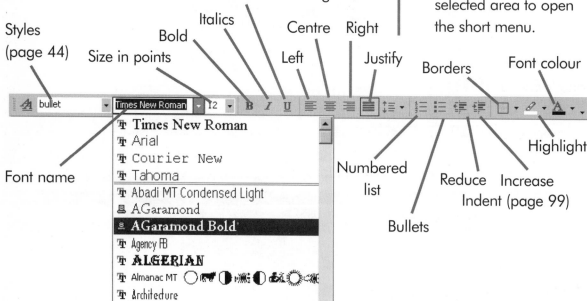

Styles (page 44)

Size in points

Bold

Italics

Underline

Left

Centre

Alignment

Right

Justify

Borders

Font colour

Highlight

Font name

Numbered list

Bullets

Reduce Indent

Increase Indent (page 99)

Fonts list:
- Times New Roman
- Arial
- Courier New
- Tahoma
- Abadi MT Condensed Light
- AGaramond
- **AGaramond Bold**
- Agency FB
- **ALGERIAN**
- Almanac MT
- Architecture
- Arial

The Fonts dialog box

There will be times when the toolbars are not enough and you need to turn to the Fonts dialog box. Use this when you want to:

- set $_{subscript,}$ ^{superscript}, and other effects;
- convert headings to FULL or SMALL CAPITALS;
- check the suitability of a **new font.**

Tip

Some fonts are larger or heavier than others of the same size and style. Always choose your font before you change any of the other settings.

4 Select Font (Format cells in Excel).

5 Switch to the Font tab if it is not already open.

6 If you are going to change the font, *do this first*.

7 Set other effects as required, checking the appearance in the Preview pane.

8 Click [OK].

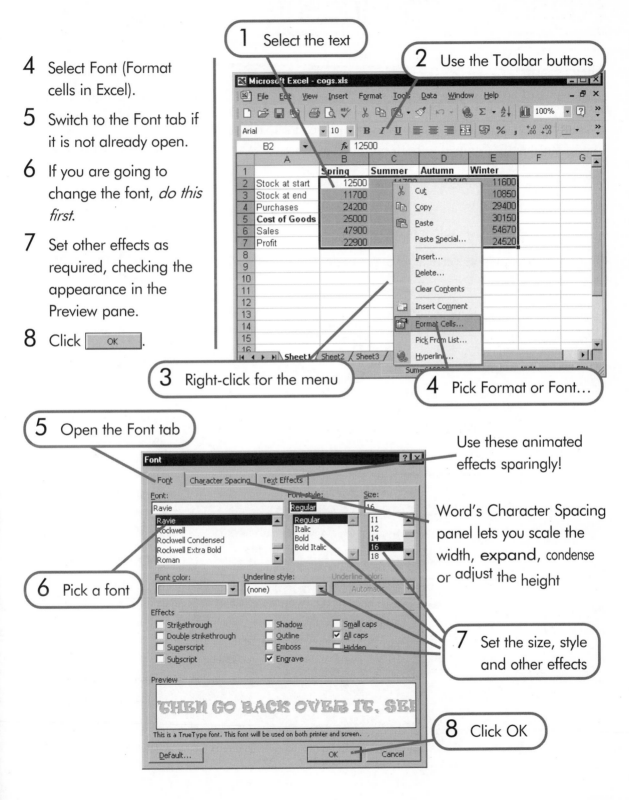

1 Select the text

2 Use the Toolbar buttons

3 Right-click for the menu

4 Pick Format or Font...

5 Open the Font tab

6 Pick a font

7 Set the size, style and other effects

8 Click OK

Use these animated effects sparingly!

Word's Character Spacing panel lets you scale the width, **expand**, condense or adjust the height

Alignment and Indents

Alignment

This refers to how text fits against the margins (or the edges of Excel cells). Four options are always available: Left, Right, Centre and Justify (aligned to both margins).

Excel also has other options to handle headings. You can:

● centre the text from one cell across a range of cells, perhaps to give a table a heading;

● set column labels vertical or at an angle.

❑ Centred headings

1 Select the cells that the text is to be centred in.

2 Click  Merge and Center.

❑ Angled text

3 Select the cells

4 Right-click and select Format Cells…

5 Switch to Alignment.

6 Rotate the Text pointer as desired.

Text in A1 centred across A1 to E1

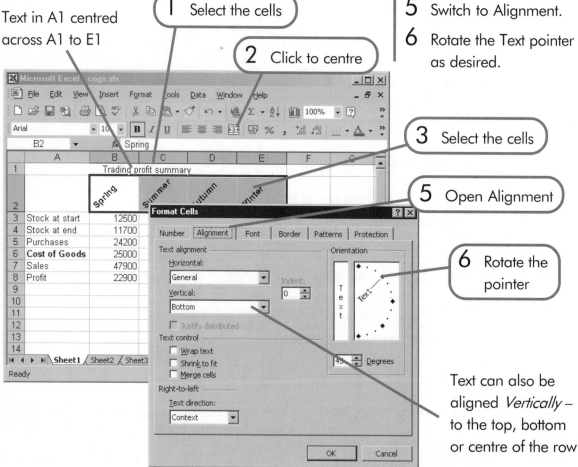

1 Select the cells

2 Click to centre

3 Select the cells

5 Open Alignment

6 Rotate the pointer

Text can also be aligned *Vertically* – to the top, bottom or centre of the row

Basic steps

1 Select the text.
2 Click ≡ to increase the indent.

Or

3 Click ≡ to pull back out.

Indents

Indents set the distance from the edge of the page margins, or of the cells in Excel. In Word and PowerPoint, they can also be used to create a structure of headings and subheadings.

Indenting is simplest with the buttons – each click pushes the text in (or out) 5mm.

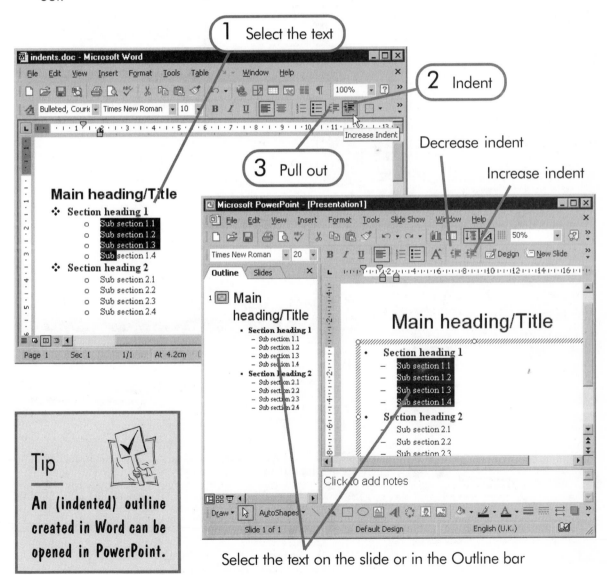

1 Select the text

2 Indent

3 Pull out

Decrease indent

Increase indent

Tip

An (indented) outline created in Word can be opened in PowerPoint.

Select the text on the slide or in the Outline bar

Bullets

In Word and PowerPoint, you can quickly add numbers or bullets to each item in a list by clicking ≡ or ≣. For finer control, use **Format – Bullets and Numbering**.

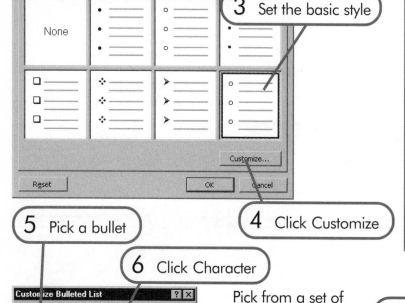

1 Select the whole list.

2 Open the Format menu and select Bullets and Numbering.

3 Select the basic style.

4 Click Customize....

5 Pick a bullet.

Or

6 Click Character... to choose a different character.

7 Select a font and subset (if required).

8 Select a character and click OK.

5 Pick a bullet

4 Click Customize

6 Click Character

Pick from a set of bullet pictures

7 Select the font and subset

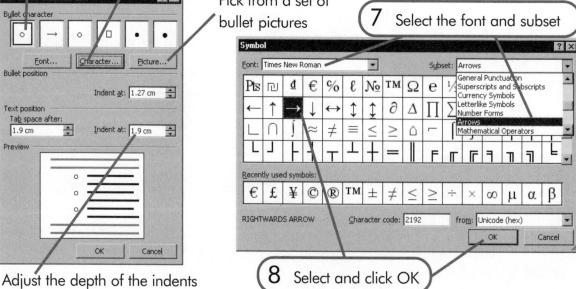

Adjust the depth of the indents

8 Select and click OK

Basic steps

- ❑ Simple numbering
- **1** Select the items.
- **2** Open the Format menu and select Bullets and Numbering.
- **3** Go to the Numbered tab and select a style.
- **4** Set the options as required.
- ❑ Outline Numbering
- **5** Start with the whole list, indented to set its structure.
- **6** Go to the Outline Numbered tab and select a style.
- **7** Click [OK].

Numbered lists

Numbered lists are basically the same in Word and PowerPoint. However, they do have different options, reflecting their different natures – a PowerPoint slide will rarely have more than two levels of numbering, but a Word document could have many levels of numbering, spread over many pages. Use Word's special **Outline Numbered** and **List Styles** tabs for styling multi-level documents.

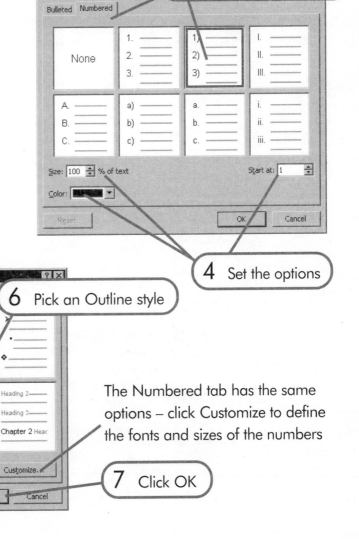

3 Pick a Numbered style

4 Set the options

6 Pick an Outline style

The Numbered tab has the same options – click Customize to define the fonts and sizes of the numbers

7 Click OK

Autoformats

When word-processors added facilities for fancy fonts and layouts, productivity in many offices took a great leap *backwards*. Instead of simply typing and printing their documents, people spent time – often too much – prettying them up. Not enough people asked themselves if it was really worth the effort. The trouble is, if you want your documents to look 'professional', plain typing will no longer do. But don't worry, here's a great leap forward. The Autoformats in Word and Excel give you attractive documents *instantly*.

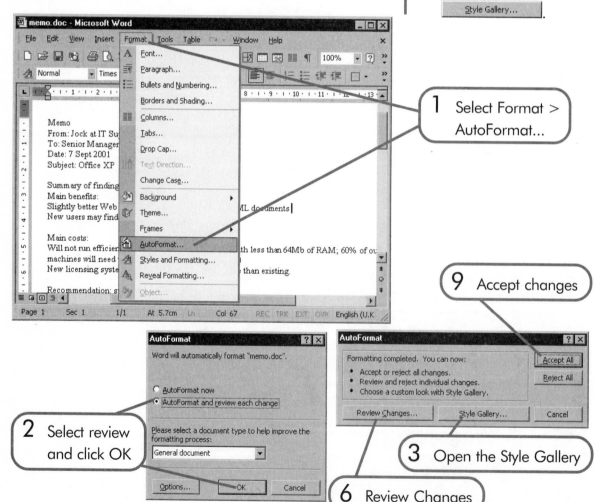

1 Select Format > AutoFormat...

2 Select review and click OK

3 Open the Style Gallery

6 Review Changes

9 Accept changes

Basic steps

4 At the Style Gallery, select a style, checking it in the preview screen.

5 Click [OK] when you find one you like.

6 Click [Review Changes...].

7 Use the Find buttons to work through the changes and [Reject] any you don't like.

8 Click [Cancel] to end the review.

9 Click [Accept All].

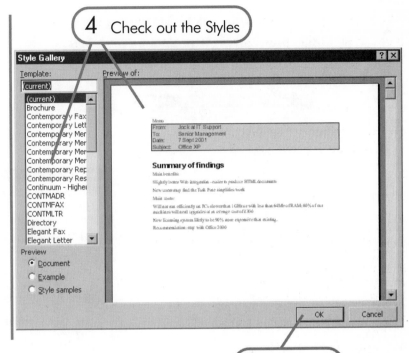

4 Check out the Styles

5 Click OK

The new format is shown here

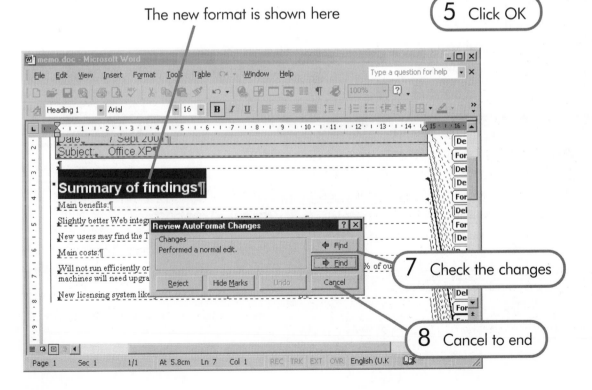

7 Check the changes

8 Cancel to end

AutoFormat Options

At some point, look at Word's **AutoFormat** options and set them to suit your preferences. If in doubt, leave options on. Later you can turn off those which do not prove to be useful.

Basic steps

1 At the Autoformat dialog box, click [Options...].

2 Check those items that you want to format.

3 Click [OK].

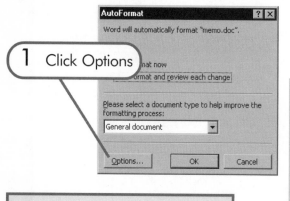

1 Click Options

Tip

Check the AutoFormat As You Type tab and turn on the options you want active when you are typing.

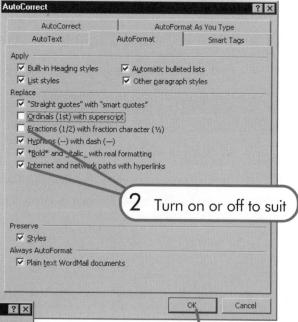

2 Turn on or off to suit

3 Click OK

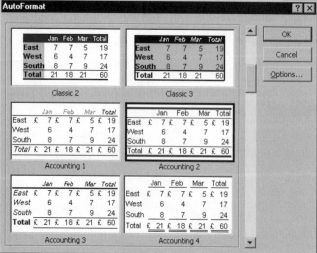

Excel AutoFormat

Excel has a wide range of ready-made formats for tables of data. Select the table, give the Format > AutoFormat command and pick a style from the list.

AutoCorrect

1 At the AutoFormat dialog box, click Options... and go to AutoCorrect.

❏ Excel and PowerPoint

2 Open the Tools menu and select AutoCorrect.

3 Put a tick by those items you want corrected.

❏ Adding to the list

4 In the document, type the text correctly and select it.

5 Go to AutoCorrect.

6 Click Plain Text.

7 Enter the error or a character combination into the Replace slot.

8 Click Add.

Don't confuse this with the Spell Checker. Both correct typing, but AutoCorrect performs a one-for-one substitution from a limited list, rather than checking against a large dictionary. Use it to:

● correct common transpositions – **teh** into **the;**

● correct common misspellings – **acheive** into **achieve;**

● call up special characters – type **(c)** and AutoCorrect swaps it for ©.

You can add your own common 'typos' or substitutions to the list if they are not already there.

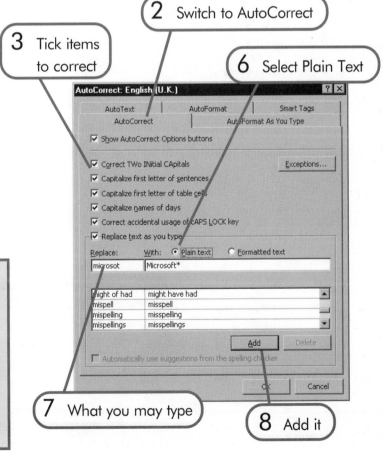

2 Switch to AutoCorrect

3 Tick items to correct

6 Select Plain Text

7 What you may type

8 Add it

Exceptions for capitalising

AutoCorrect also checks that the first letters of sentences are capitals. As a sentence is defined as something that comes after a full stop, abbreviations can create problems. The solution is to have a list of abbreviations and not capitalise words that follow them. You can add to this list.

Are the other Capital rules right for you?

Basic steps

1 Open the AutoCorrect dialog box and click ⌊Exceptions...⌋.

2 Switch to the First Letter tab.

3 Type your new abbreviation in the Don't Capitalize After slot.

4 Click ⌊Add⌋.

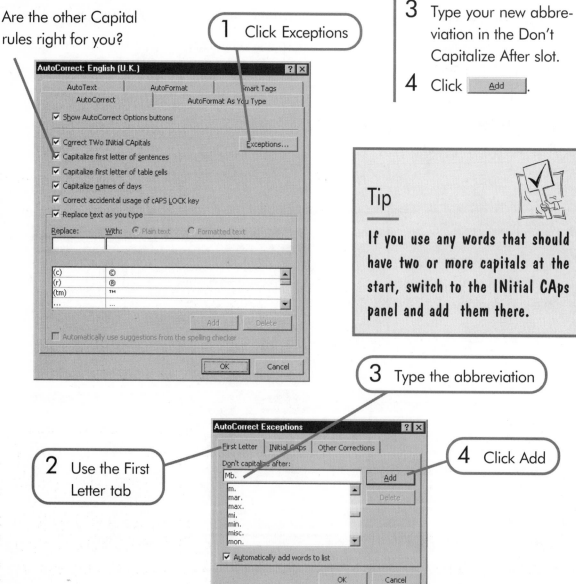

1 Click Exceptions

2 Use the First Letter tab

3 Type the abbreviation

4 Click Add

Tip

If you use any words that should have two or more capitals at the start, switch to the INitial CAps panel and add them there.

Basic steps

Undoing one action

1 Click the arrow on the Undo button 🔄▾.

Undoing several actions

2 Open the list from the Undo button 🔄▾.

3 Point down the list to highlight all the actions that you want to undo and click.

Undo

In the old days, you were lucky if your software allowed you to undo a mistake. With the Office applications you can go back and undo a whole string of actions. This doesn't just protect you from the results of hasty decisions or self-willed mice, it gives you a freedom to experiment. You can do major editing or reformatting, and if at the end you preferred things how they were, you can undo your way back to it.

● You cannot undo one action from part-way down the list – all those above are also undone.

Redo

This is the un-undo button! If you undo too much, use this to put it back again. Use it for one or several actions, like Undo.

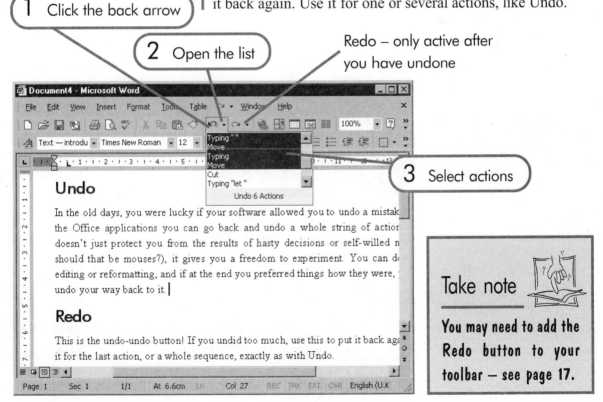

1 Click the back arrow

2 Open the list

Redo – only active after you have undone

3 Select actions

Take note

You may need to add the Redo button to your toolbar – see page 17.

Spelling

Spell checking is present in all Office applications. There is a good dictionary behind it, but it does not cover everything. Proper names, technical and esoteric words may be unrecognised and thrown up as 'errors'. These can be added to your own dictionary, so that they are not seen as errors in future.

Word and PowerPoint have a check-as-you-type option. You may prefer to just run a spell check after you have finished – especially if you have a lot to do and need to watch the keyboard rather than the screen!

1 If you want to check part of a document, or a block of cells in a spreadsheet, select it.

2 Open the Tools menu and select Spelling or click 🔤.

❏ When a word is not recognised you can:

3 Select a Suggestion and click [Change].

or

4 If it is a valid word click [Ignore Once] or [Ignore All] .

or

5 [Add to Dictionary] to put it in a custom dictionary.

or

6 Click in the Not in Dictionary slot, edit the word then click [Change].

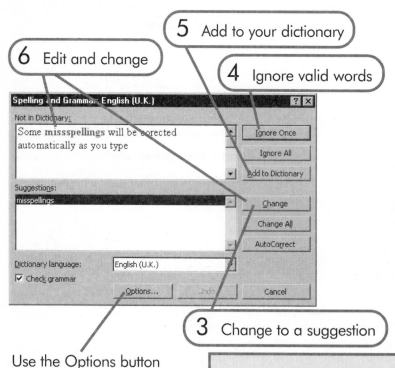

5 Add to your dictionary

6 Edit and change

4 Ignore valid words

3 Change to a suggestion

Use the Options button to set your preferences (see opposite)

Take note

If you haven't already set up a dictionary for your own special words, click the Options button to open the Spelling options panel and use the Custom Dictionaries button.

Basic steps

1 On the Spelling dialog box, click Options.

2 Turn the settings on or off as desired.

❑ Fine-tuning grammar

3 Click Settings....

4 In Writing style, select *Grammar Only* or *Grammar and Style*.

5 Turn other checks on or off as desired.

6 Click OK.

Check as you type?

Use this to find out how readable your text is. For an adult audience, aim for a readability of Grade 7 (a reading age of 12) – any lower is patronising; higher is hard work for most people.

Spelling and grammar options

Probably the key options here are whether or not to check spelling and grammar as you type – some people will find that it interrupts their flow, while others prefer to correct errors as they go.

Use this if you want to create specialist dictionaries for different types of jobs

2 Set options

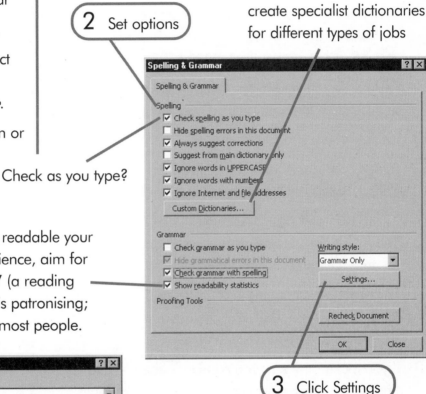

3 Click Settings

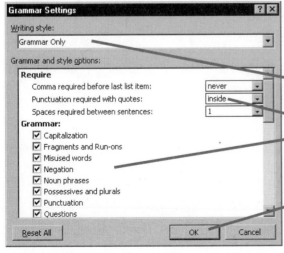

4 Also check the style?

5 Set options

6 Click OK

109

Summary

- ❑ Text can be selected with either the mouse or keys, or a combination of both. Objects can be selected by clicking on them, or dragging an outline round them with the mouse. The same selection techniques apply in all applications.

- ❑ Font types, sizes and styles can be set from the Formatting toolbar or the Fonts dialog box. The dialog box also has additional control options.

- ❑ Text can be aligned to the Left or Right margins, Centred between them or Justified up to both.

- ❑ Indents give a structure to text.

- ❑ Bullets or numbers can be easily added to lists. The default bullets can be replaced by any characters you choose; numbers can be set in various styles.

- ❑ The Autoformat facility gives you standard formats for common documents and tables of data.

- ❑ The AutoCorrect routine recognises and corrects mistakes as you type. This may need customising to stop it 'correcting' intentional irregularities.

- ❑ If you make mistakes, you can Undo them – and if you undo too many actions, you can Redo them again!

- ❑ The Spelling checker has a good dictionary, and you can build your own to hold special terms and names that are not in the main one.

7 Other objects

Importing pictures

'A picture is worth a thousand words.' That philosophy can be applied to many types of documents.

● Your company logo will identify your letter and invoices;

● Products sell better if people can see pictures of them;

● Diagrams are often essential for communicating technical information and other complex concepts.

Basic steps

1 Open the Insert menu, point to Picture then select From File...

Or

2 Click on the Picture toolbar.

3 Switch to the picture's folder.

4 If there are lots, use the Files of type box to filter out the right type.

5 Pick a picture, checking its preview.

6 Click [Insert].

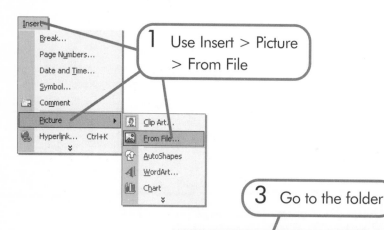

1 Use Insert > Picture > From File

3 Go to the folder

Tip

JPG, GIF, Photo CD and other graphics files can be imported if you have installed the graphic converter routines for them.

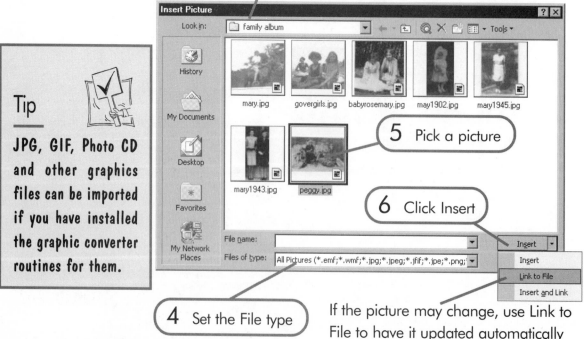

5 Pick a picture

6 Click Insert

4 Set the File type

If the picture may change, use Link to File to have it updated automatically

Basic steps

1 Use Insert > Picture > Clip Art... to open Insert Clip Art in the Task Pane.

2 Type the Search For word(s).

3 Drop down the Results should be list and tick the types of media that you want.

4 Click Search .

5 Scroll through the results to find a picture.

6 To insert it, double-click or click the arrow bar and select Insert.

Clip art

Clip art pictures can be inserted into any application – but don't overdo it. There's so much clip art around that you must use it selectively to have any impact.

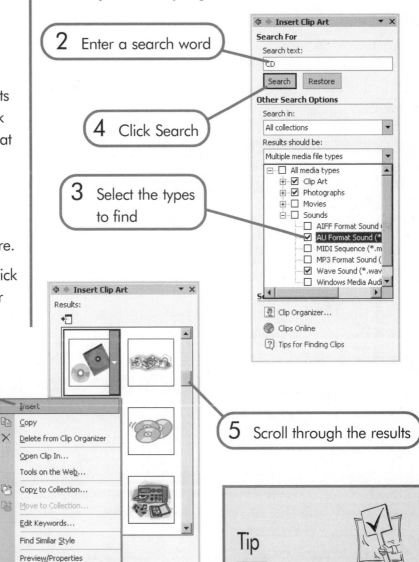

2 Enter a search word

4 Click Search

3 Select the types to find

6 Click Insert

5 Scroll through the results

Preview sounds, video clips, animated GIFs and similar files

Tip

You will need the Media CD in the drive to preview or insert the clips.

Clip Organizer

The Clip Organizer can help you to keep track of your clip art, video and sound clips, pictures, photographs – in fact, just about any type of multimedia file.

When first installed, the Clip Organizer only knows about the media files on the Office CD. These are organised into collections – which is just as well as there are thousands of them! Browse through the collections as you would browse through the folders on a disk.

1 With Insert Clip Art open in the Task Pane, click the Clip Organizer link.

2 Browse through the collections.

3 To preview a file, click the arrow bar and select Preview.

4 If the file is on the CD and you want a more accessible copy, use Copy to Collection to add it to a folder in the My Collections list.

2 Browse the clips

3 Preview a clip

4 Copy to a collection on your hard disk

If the file is on your hard disk, you can define its keywords

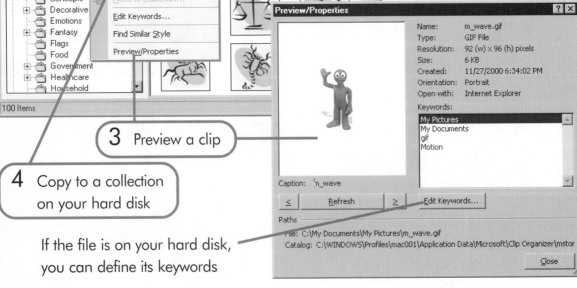

114

Organising your media files

1 Open the File menu,
   point to Add Clips to
   Organizer and click
   On My Own...

2 Set the Look in folder.

3 Select the files to add.

4 Click Add To... and
   select the collection.

Or

5 Click Add to add them
   to the Unclassified
   collection.

If you tell the Clip Organizer about your files, it will make it easier to find them when you later want to insert them into documents. There are two ways of doing this:

● **Automatically** will search through your hard drive for any suitable file types and add them to the Unclassified collection. This is not advised if you have more than a few dozen files.

● Using **On My Own...** you can select the files that you want to add and put them in a collection at the same time.

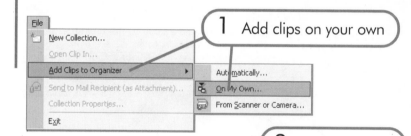

1 Add clips on your own

2 Set the folder

3 Select the clips

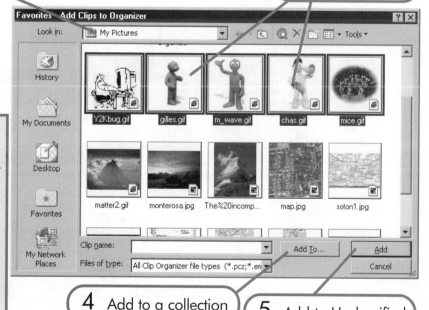

4 Add to a collection

5 Add to Unclassified

Take note

The clips from your hard disk can be moved to other collections at any point – use the option on their short menu.

Formatting pictures

The final appearance of any picture – clip art, file, drawing or diagram – can be adjusted at any point. Use the mouse to change the size, shape or position, or use the Picture toolbar or the Format Picture dialog box to add an outline, crop it, adjust the colours, or set how text wraps around it.

Basic steps

1. Select the picture.

2. Drag a handle to adjust the size.

3. Drag anywhere within the area to move.

4. Use the Picture tools to adjust the settings.

Or

5. Right-click and select Format Picture, then work through the panels – you can adjust some settings more accurately here.

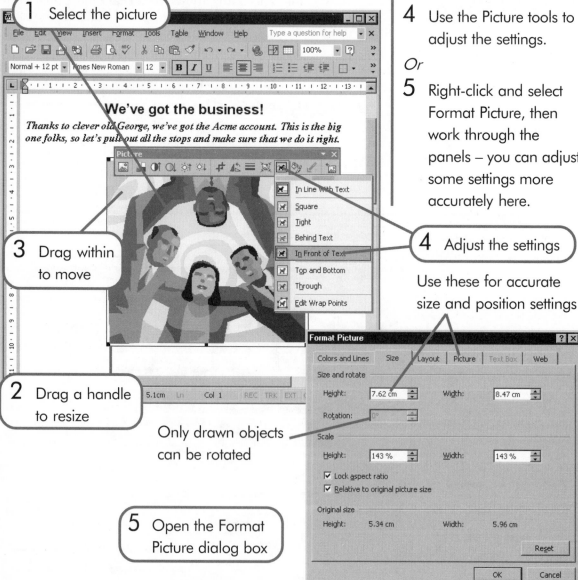

1 Select the picture

We've got the business!

Thanks to clever old George, we've got the Acme account. This is the big one folks, so let's pull out all the stops and make sure that we do it right.

In Line With Text
Square
Tight
Behind Text
In Front of Text
Top and Bottom
Through
Edit Wrap Points

3 Drag within to move

4 Adjust the settings

Use these for accurate size and position settings

2 Drag a handle to resize

Only drawn objects can be rotated

Format Picture

Colors and Lines | Size | Layout | Picture | Text Box | Web

Size and rotate

Height: 7.62 cm   Width: 8.47 cm

Rotation: 0°

Scale

Height: 143 %   Width: 143 %

☑ Lock aspect ratio
☑ Relative to original picture size

Original size

Height: 5.34 cm   Width: 5.96 cm

Reset

OK   Cancel

5 Open the Format Picture dialog box

116

The Picture toolbar

Tip

You can get more clips from the Web — just click the Clips Online shortcut.

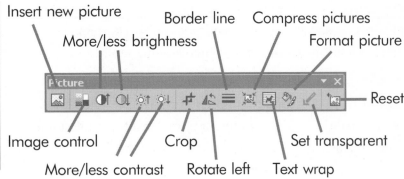

- Insert new picture
- More/less brightness
- Border line
- Compress pictures
- Format picture
- Reset
- Image control
- More/less contrast
- Crop
- Rotate left
- Set transparent
- Text wrap

Grayscale

Black & White

We've got the business!

Thanks to clever old George, we've got the Acme account. This is the big one folks, so let's pull out all the stops and make sure that we do it right.

Washout, used here as a background

Image control

The Image control menu gives you four options:

Automatic – in its normal colours;

Grayscale – for output to black-only printers, use with photographs and complex images;

Black & White – for high-contrast black-only printing, use with line-drawings or for special effects;

Washout – ultra-pale, for use as background images.

Compress pictures

Sets the options for storing images in compressed format. If you may later want to copy the images out of the document, do not compress them as you may lose definition.

Text wrap

This defines how the picture fits with nearby text – it can be surrounded by it, behind it, above it, or in a clear space of its own.

Set transparent

Select this and click on a colour, and that colour will become transparent so that the background shows through. It's much used on Web pages for non-rectangular logos and images.

Drawing pictures

If you want to create new images, pick out points on imported pictures, or add arrows, blobs or blocks of background colour, there is a handy set of tools on the Drawing toolbar.

In a drawn picture, each item remains separate and can be moved, resized, recoloured or deleted at any later time. (Though items can be joined into Groups or placed inside picture frames, for convenient handling.) This is quite different from Paint and similar packages, where each addition becomes merged permanently into the whole picture.

The Draw menu lets you manipulate elements, singly or in groups

Basic steps

1 Click ☝ to open the Drawing toolbar.

2 Select an object tool and point and drag to create the item.

3 Adjust the fill and line colour and style.

4 To adjust an item, use the Selector tool and click on it. It can then be moved, resized, deleted or recoloured.

5 Double-click on an element to open its Format dialog box for fine-tuning its display.

Selector

Autoshapes offer a quick way to get neat effects

Basic lines and shapes

Fill and line colours

Line and arrow styles

Callout – a text box with a speech/thought bubble outline

Cylinder Autoshape

Rectangle

Ovals

Line

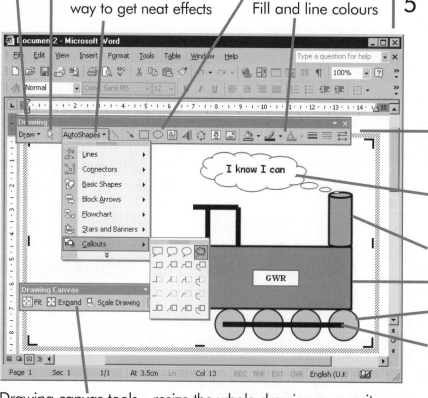

Drawing canvas tools – resize the whole drawing as a unit

118

The drop-down palette has the basic colours, and access to the full palette (More Fill Colors…).

Fill Effects include Gradients and Textures – use them both for the backgrounds of boxes.

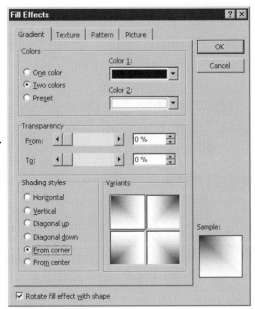

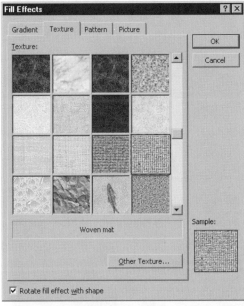

Patterned Lines are reached from the Line Colour panel. Try them for distinctive frames.

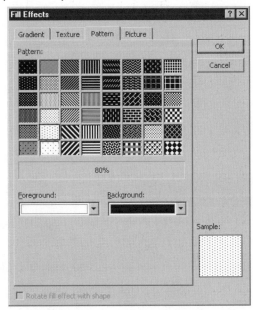

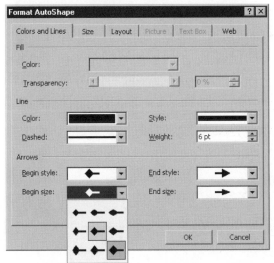

Add arrowheads from the Format dialog box – double-click on a line to open this.

Diagrams

Office XP offers six types of ready-made diagram outlines.

- Organization Chart
- Cycle
- Radial
- Pyramid
- Venn
- Target

Cycle, radial, pyramid, venn and target are interchangeable, so that a diagram which started life as a radial could be changed into a pyramid after its data had been added and formatting applied.

Basic steps

1 Click ⬚ on the Drawing toolbar.

Or

2 Open the Insert menu and select Diagram.

3 Select a Diagram type.

4 Click ⬚OK⬚.

5 Replace the prompt text and add more shapes as needed.

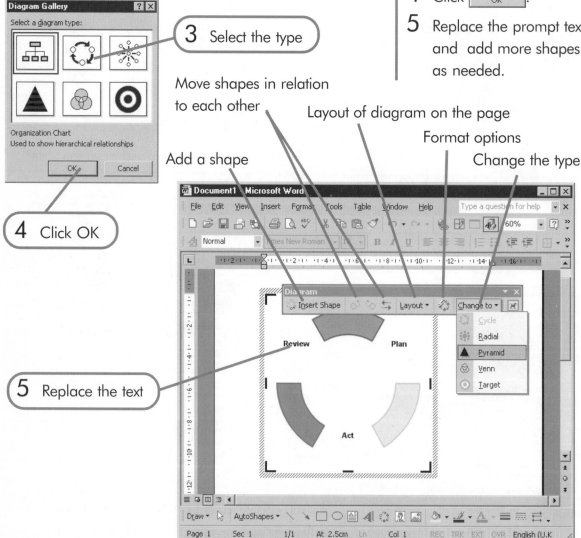

3 Select the type

4 Click OK

Move shapes in relation to each other

Layout of diagram on the page

Format options

Add a shape

Change the type

5 Replace the text

120

Basic steps

1 Start as on page 120, and select Organization Chart at step 3.

2 Replace the prompts with names and/or titles as required.

❑ To add a box

3 Click the box to which the new one will be added.

4 Click Insert Shape to add a subordinate.

Or

5 Drop down the list to select a different relationship.

❑ To delete a box

6 Click on it and press [Delete].

Organization Chart

The concept behind organization charts is simple. A chart consists of boxes containing the name, title and comments for each person. They can be linked to each other in different ways to indicate the nature of the relationship. Starting from the basic boss + three underlings, you can add boxes for three types of relationships to build a chart for your organisation.

● These charts can have more complex structures than the other diagrams and are not interchangeable with them.

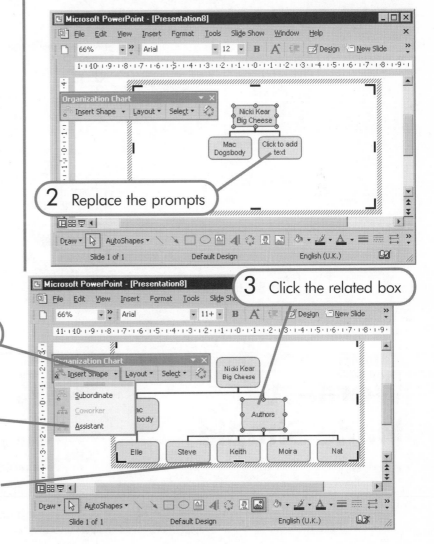

2 Replace the prompts

3 Click the related box

4 Click Insert Shape

5 Select a relationship

Four authors have been added as subordinates to the 'Authors' box

WordArt

If you want a fancy front cover for a report, or a high impact slide, you might like to investigate WordArt. It has some excellent facilities, but is very easy to use. With it, you can shape and style text in ways that go far beyond the standard Font Formatting tools.

Basic steps

1 Open the Insert menu and select Picture then WordArt.

2 Select a style from the Gallery.

3 Click [OK].

4 Enter your text at the prompt.

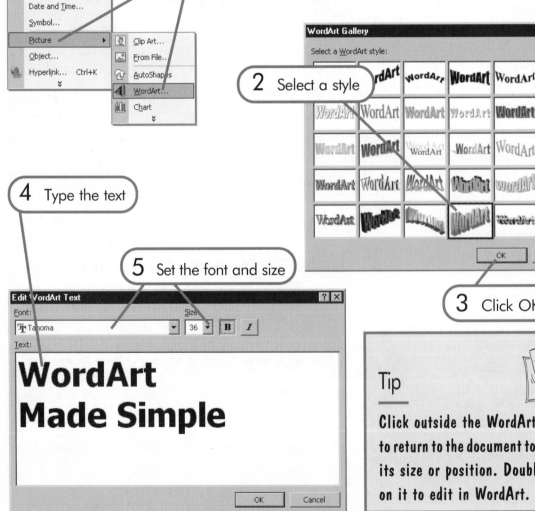

1 Use Insert > Picture > WordArt

2 Select a style

3 Click OK

4 Type the text

5 Set the font and size

WordArt
Made Simple

Tip

Click outside the WordArt object to return to the document to change its size or position. Double-click on it to edit in WordArt.

122

5   Set the font and size.

6   Use the tools to adjust the shape, colour and other effects.

7   Click outside the WordArt area to end.

All letters the same size
Vertical text
WordArt Gallery (as at Step 2)
Text Wrap
Alignment

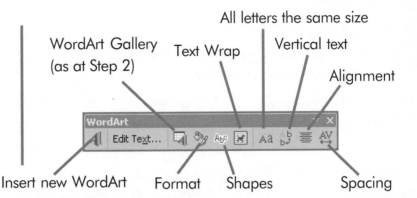

Insert new WordArt   Format   Shapes   Spacing

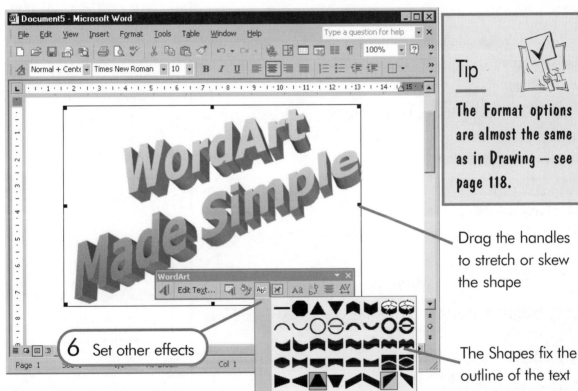

6   Set other effects

Tip

The Format options are almost the same as in Drawing – see page 118.

Drag the handles to stretch or skew the shape

The Shapes fix the outline of the text

Alignment options set the lines of text within the overall shape

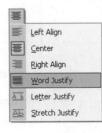

Spacing options are mainly used where there are several lines of text

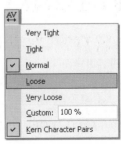

Tables

If you need to lay out data in neat columns and rows in Word or PowerPoint, the simplest way to do it is with a table. But tables can also be used for more than this.

You don't have to stick to a fixed grid – rows and columns can be varied in size, and cells can run across two or more cells or columns. This means that you can use a table as the framework for a display, ensuring that each element sits in the right place on the screen – this can be very useful when creating Web pages or non-standard PowerPoint slides.

In Word, there are additional Table tools that can be used to add sets of figures, or to sort rows or columns into ascending or descending order.

If you want to create a simple regular table, use the 🔲 tool or the Insert > Table command. If necessary, rows and columns can be added or deleted later, or cells merged or split to produce more complex layouts.

If the table is to be used for layout, the ✏️ tool will let you draw the outline and dividers where you want them.

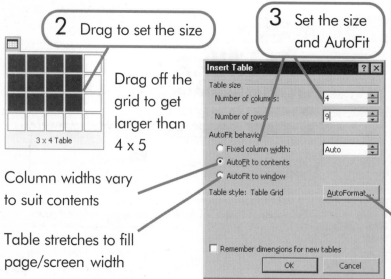

2 Drag to set the size

Drag off the grid to get larger than 4 x 5

3 x 4 Table

Column widths vary to suit contents

Table stretches to fill page/screen width

3 Set the size and AutoFit

□ **Simple tables**

1 Place the cursor where the table is to go.

2 Click 🔲 and drag the highlight across the grid to set the size.

Or

3 Use Insert>– Table (in PowerPoint) or Table > Insert > Table (Word) and set the size and AutoFit option.

□ **Drawn tables**

4 Use Table > Draw Table or click ✏️ on the Tables and Borders toolbar.

5 Draw the table outline.

6 Draw lines across or down where needed – across the table or between existing lines.

7 Click ✏️ again to turn the drawing mode off.

8 Enter the data into the cells, formatting the text as normal.

Almost the same as Excel AutoFormats – see page 60

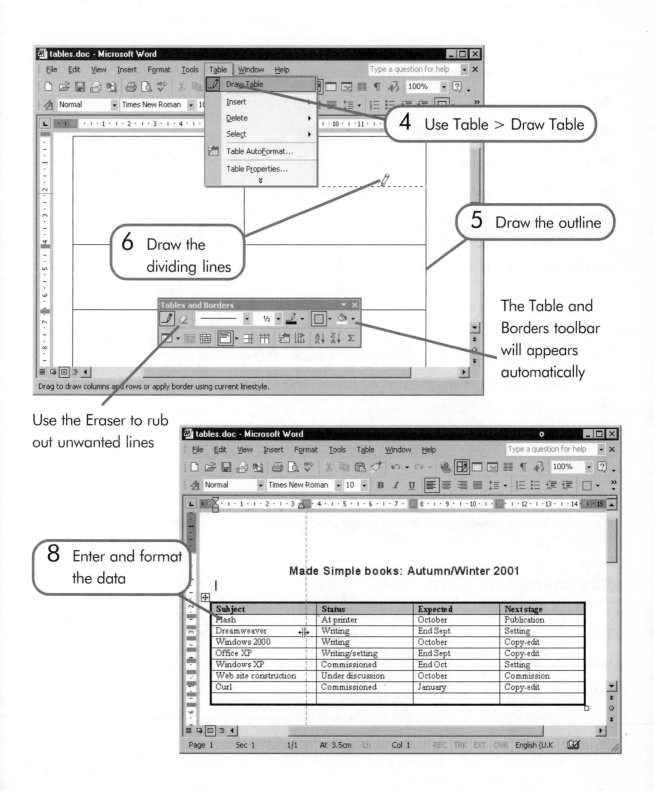

4 Use Table > Draw Table

5 Draw the outline

6 Draw the dividing lines

The Table and Borders toolbar will appears automatically

Use the Eraser to rub out unwanted lines

8 Enter and format the data

Made Simple books: Autumn/Winter 2001

Subject	Status	Expected	Next stage
Flash	At printer	October	Publication
Dreamweaver	Writing	End Sept	Setting
Windows 2000	Writing	October	Copy-edit
Office XP	Writing/setting	End Sept	Copy-edit
Windows XP	Commissioned	End Oct	Setting
Web site construction	Under discussion	October	Commission
Curl	Commissioned	January	Copy-edit

Modifying tables

A table's size, shape and layout can be changed at any time – even after data has been entered into it. You can:

- Insert or delete rows or columns;

- Split a cell into two or more rows or columns;

- Merge cells into one, across rows or columns.

In Word, the commands can all be found on the **Table** menu, with most also present on the **Tables and Borders** toolbar.

PowerPoint has a more limited set of commands, and these can only be reached through its **Tables and Borders** toolbar.

❏ Inserting rows/columns

1 Select a row/column adjacent to where the new one will go.

2 Select an Insert option from the Table menu.

❏ Deleting rows/columns

3 Select the rows/columns.

4 Select a Delete option from the Table menu.

❏ Merging cells

5 Select the cells and click 🗗.

Or

6 Select the Eraser 🖉 and rub out the line(s).

❏ Splitting cells

7 Select the cell and click 🗗 then enter the new number of rows or columns.

Or

8 Select 🖉 and draw the line(s).

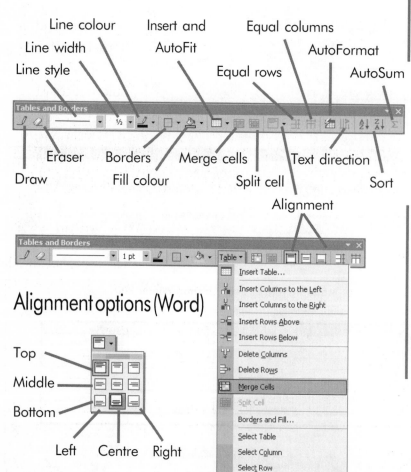

Line colour
Line width
Line style
Insert and AutoFit
Equal columns
Equal rows
AutoFormat
AutoSum

Eraser   Borders   Merge cells   Text direction
Draw   Fill colour   Split cell   Sort
Alignment

Alignment options (Word)

Top
Middle
Bottom

Left   Centre   Right

Insert Table...
Insert Columns to the Left
Insert Columns to the Right
Insert Rows Above
Insert Rows Below
Delete Columns
Delete Rows
Merge Cells
Split Cell
Borders and Fill...
Select Table
Select Column
Select Row

Basic steps

❑ Borders

1 Select the cells.

2 Set the line style, width and colour.

3 Click the Border tool and select the lines to be styled.

4 Repeat steps 2 and 3 for other lines.

Formatting tables

Text in cells can be formatted as normal. You can also:

● set the vertical and horizontal alignment of cell contents;

● format the borders and the lines within the table – you can format the various lines differently (see the Steps);

● change the background colour of selected cells.

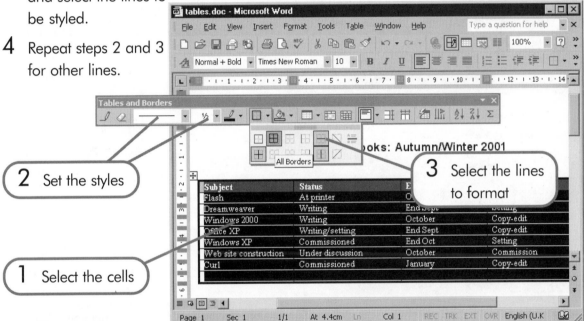

2 Set the styles

1 Select the cells

3 Select the lines to format

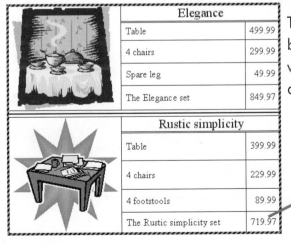

Elegance	
Table	499.99
4 chairs	299.99
Spare leg	49.99
The Elegance set	849.97

Rustic simplicity	
Table	399.99
4 chairs	229.99
4 footstools	89.99
The Rustic simplicity set	719.97

Table used mainly for layout – this was drawn, but could have been started as a 10 × 3 grid, with cells merged across rows on the left, and across columns for the two titles.

Total found by selecting this cell and clicking AutoSum to add the column of figures above it (it can also add a row to its left)

Quick graphs

If you want to knock up a quick chart or graph in a Word or PowerPoint document, the Graph Chart software will do the job. It gives you a datasheet and related graph, set up with dummy data. All you have to do is replace that data with your own. If you care to spend the time, you can also change the chart style, colours and other aspects of its appearance.

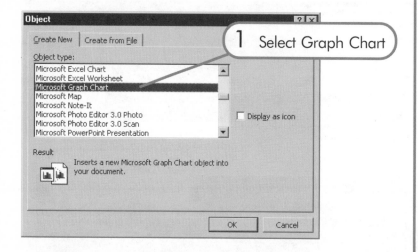

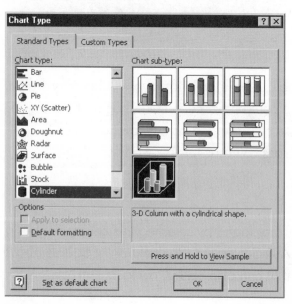

Basic steps

1 Open the Insert menu, select Object then Graph Chart.

2 Type your data into the datasheet, adding more columns or rows if needed.

3 Use the tools to change the display – most toggle features on and off.

4 Select an item from the chart and right-click for its formatting options.

Or

5 Select the element from the drop-down list and click the Formatting button.

6 Click back into the document and adjust the graph's size.

The default chart is an upright bar style, but you have plenty of choice! There is a full range of normal chart types on the Standard tab – and some striking ones on the Custom tab.

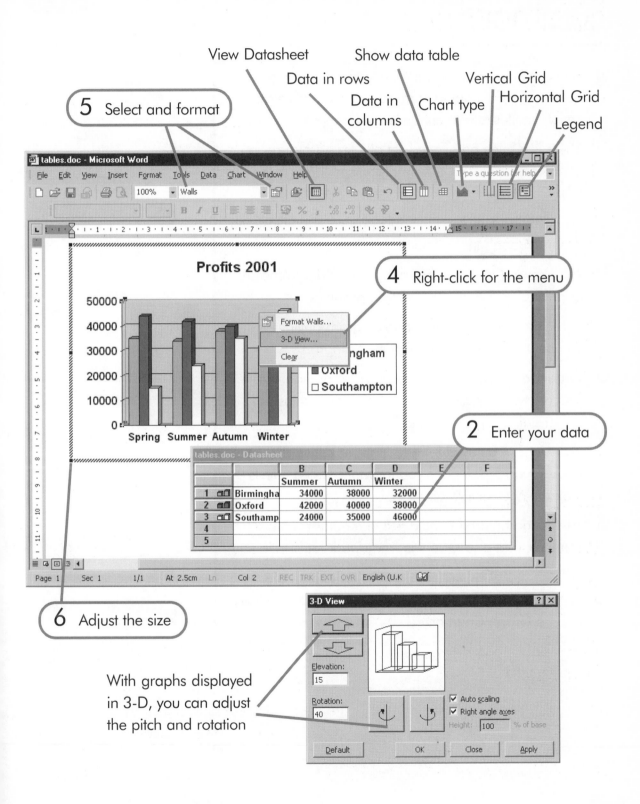

View Datasheet

Show data table

Data in rows

Vertical Grid

5 Select and format

Data in columns

Chart type

Horizontal Grid

Legend

tables.doc - Microsoft Word

File Edit View Insert Format Tools Data Chart Window Help

Type a question for help

100% Walls

Profits 2001

4 Right-click for the menu

50000

40000

Format Walls...

30000

3-D View...

ngham

Clear

Oxford

20000

Southampton

10000

0

Spring Summer Autumn Winter

2 Enter your data

tables.doc - Datasheet

			B	C	D	E	F
			Summer	Autumn	Winter		
1	📊	Birmingha	34000	38000	32000		
2	📊	Oxford	42000	40000	38000		
3	📊	Southamp	24000	35000	46000		
4							
5							

Page 1   Sec 1   1/1   At 2.5cm Ln   Col 2   REC TRK EXT OVR English (U.K

6 Adjust the size

3-D View

With graphs displayed
in 3-D, you can adjust
the pitch and rotation

Elevation:
15

Rotation:
40

☑ Auto scaling
☑ Right angle axes
Height: 100   % of base

Default   OK   Close   Apply

Summary

❑ You can import clip art, pictures and other images in most common graphics formats into any Office application, to illustrate or enhance a document.

❑ There is a huge and varied set of Clip Art pictures on the media CD. Clips can be organised through the Clip Organizer.

❑ You can fine-tune the final appearance of any inserted picture through the Formatting options.

❑ The Drawing tools can be used to creat diagrams or add lines, arrows or other simple graphics.

❑ There are a set of ready-made diagram outlines that can be used to produce a range of diagrams.

❑ Organization charts are a special type of diagram, and are typically used to show the relationships between staff in organisations.

❑ WordArt can be used for headings, splashes and background text. It gives you far more varied effects than the normal formatting tools.

❑ Tables can be used to hold text in regular rows or columns, and also to set the framework for positioning text and images.

❑ To produce a graph from a small table of data quickly, insert a Graph Chart object.

8 Sharing data

Alternative approaches

There are a number of different ways to share data between applications. The first three bring a selected object or block of data into a second application. They use the Edit Copy and Paste commands in various ways.

- **Simple paste** – the text, table, picture or whatever, becomes an integral part of the host document, dropping all connection to the application in which it was created. Use this method where the host document's application can handle any editing or reformatting that you might want to do to the pasted-in data.

- **Embedding** – the pasted-in data forms an independent object within the document. It loses its connection to the original data, but can be edited by its own application *within the host document*. Use this method if you want to be able to edit the object using its original application.

- **Linking** – the pasted-in data retains a full connection to the original data and its application. Any changes in the source data are automatically reflected in the copy, and the original file can be edited – by calling up its application – from within the host document. This is the method to use for reports and presentations where you want to ensure that all the data is up to date.

The Copy and Paste commands work by means of the Clipboard, an area of memory separate from any application. Data stored in the Clipboard from within one application can then be accessed from within any other. If necessary it can be converted into a new format for the target application. There are a few situations where Copy and Paste will not work between applications because of fundamental differences in formats, but there is never a problem in copying data between any Office applications.

Take note

Most of the methods described here use Object Linking and Embedding (OLE). This is a standard Windows facility that can be used for sharing data between any applications.

Copy and Paste

The first step is to go to the source document, select the object or block of text and copy it, using either the **Edit > Copy** or 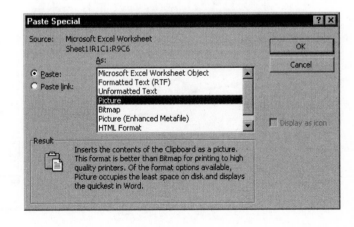.
What you do then depends upon whether you want to copy, embed or link the data, and what format you want it in.

- Use or **Edit > Paste** to copy in the data. It will normally come in with its original formatting, but alternative copy options are available.

- Use **Edit > Paste Special** to embed or link, or to select your own format for copied data.

Paste Special formats

The range of formats, and whether or not the data can be linked depends upon the source application and the nature of the data.

- **Word, Excel, PowerPoint** (or other) **Object** – use this for embedding;

- **Formatted Text** – the text retains its fonts, styles, etc., but may be edited by the host application;

- **Unformatted Text** – plain text, editable by the host;

- **Picture** and **Bitmap** – Picture give better printed images.

- **HTML** – use when creating Web pages.

When an item is pasted in, this button appears. Click the down arrow to select an option. The button is removed as soon as you do any editing on the document.

Copying

Using the and buttons is the quickest and simplest way to get data from one application into another, but the data is pasted differently in different applications.

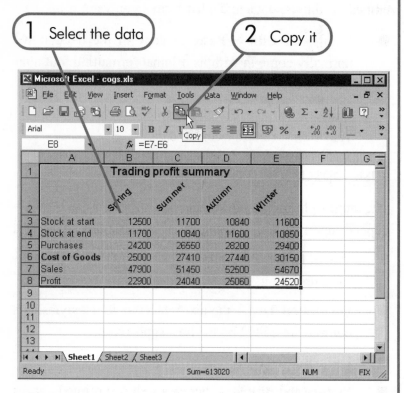

1 Select the data

2 Copy it

3 Copy to the Clipboard

6 Paste into place

1 In the source document, select the object or block of text or cells to be copied.

2 Click .

Or

3 Pull down the Edit menu and select Copy.

4 Go to the target document and point the cursor to where the data is to be placed.

5 Click .

Or

6 Pull down the Edit menu and select Paste.

7 Click the Paste Options button and select a special paste setting if required.

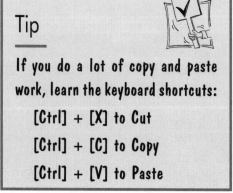

Tip

If you do a lot of copy and paste work, learn the keyboard shortcuts:

[Ctrl] + [X] to Cut

[Ctrl] + [C] to Copy

[Ctrl] + [V] to Paste

Excel to Word

A simple paste brings in the data in Rich Text Format, and creates a Word table. The options allow you to:

- format the data as it was in Excel, or apply the Word document's table style, or set it as plain text;

- retain a link to the source Excel worksheet.

Take note

Rich Text Format is a standard way of copying formatted text between many different kinds of applications — not just those in the Office set.

4 Position the cursor

5 Click Paste

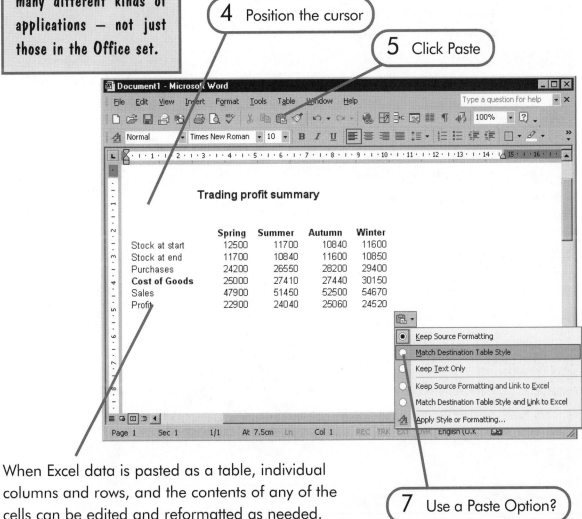

Trading profit summary

	Spring	Summer	Autumn	Winter
Stock at start	12500	11700	10840	11600
Stock at end	11700	10840	11600	10850
Purchases	24200	26550	28200	29400
Cost of Goods	25000	27410	27440	30150
Sales	47900	51450	52500	54670
Profit	22900	24040	25060	24520

- Keep Source Formatting
- Match Destination Table Style
- Keep Text Only
- Keep Source Formatting and Link to Excel
- Match Destination Table Style and Link to Excel
- Apply Style or Formatting...

When Excel data is pasted as a table, individual columns and rows, and the contents of any of the cells can be edited and reformatted as needed.

7 Use a Paste Option?

135

PowerPoint to Word

If you select all the objects on a slide at once, then Paste them, they come in as a single drawing, which can be moved or scaled as a unit. The component objects can also be moved or scaled separately and the text can be edited.

If the objects are going to illustrate a Word document, use Paste Special, and bring them in as a Picture for easier handling.

PowerPoint text typically has HUGE font sizes. When pasting into Word, the default setting applies Word's much smaller formatting. The **Keep Source Formatting** option is there, should it be required.

A group of objects will be pasted in as a drawing.

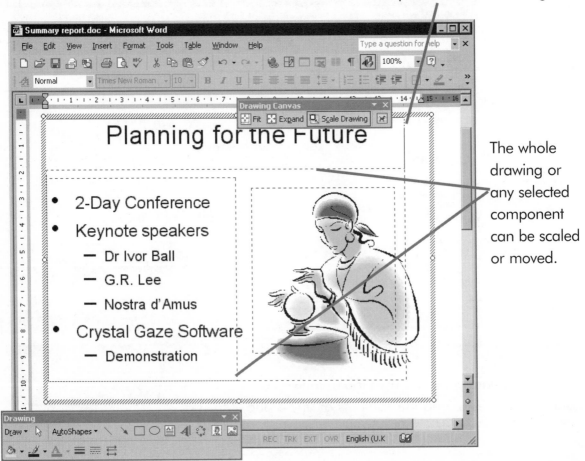

The whole drawing or any selected component can be scaled or moved.

Word to PowerPoint

❑ If you 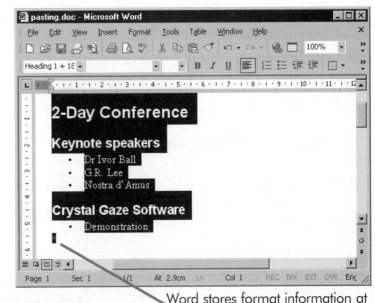 Word text onto a blank area, it will be dropped into a text box. You can accept the default PowerPoint formatting, or use the Paste Option to retain the formatting from Word.

❑ If you Paste into a *Click to add text* area of a bullet list, the text will have bullets added.

Word stores format information at the end of paragraphs – copy an extra line to make sure you have it

When pasting in text – you can retain Word's formatting

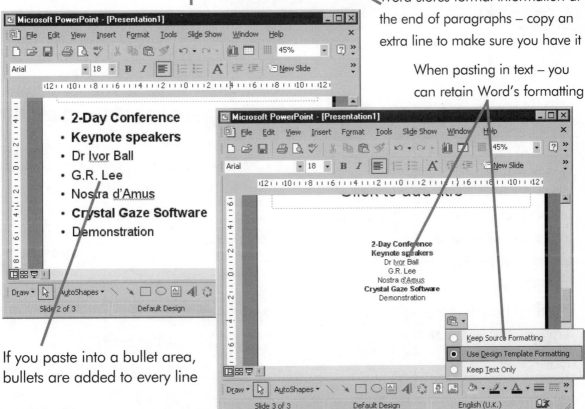

If you paste into a bullet area, bullets are added to every line

Embedding

Sometimes a simple Paste embeds an object – e.g. an Excel table in a PowerPoint slide – but to be certain that an object is embedded, it is best use the Paste Special command.

Basic steps

1 Select the object to be pasted.

2 In the target document, use Edit > Paste Special…

3 Set the As option to an Object of the original application.

4 Select Paste.

5 Click [OK].

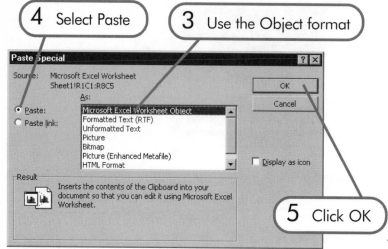

4 Select Paste

3 Use the Object format

Paste Special

Source: Microsoft Excel Worksheet
Sheet1!R1C1:R8C5

As:

◉ Paste:
○ Paste link:

Microsoft Excel Worksheet Object
Formatted Text (RTF)
Unformatted Text
Picture
Bitmap
Picture (Enhanced Metafile)
HTML Format

OK
Cancel

☐ Display as icon

Result

Inserts the contents of the Clipboard into your document so that you can edit it using Microsoft Excel Worksheet.

5 Click OK

When you edit an embedded object, the menus and toolbars change to suit the object.

Take note

The embedded object is only a copy of the original data. If you edit an embedded object, it does not affect the data in the original file and vice versa.

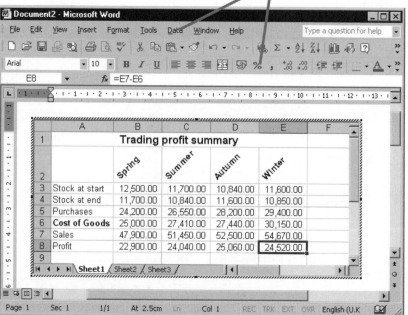

Editing embedded objects

❑ **Edit within the host**

1 Double-click on the object to open a limited version.

Or

2 Right-click to open the short menu and choose Object – Edit.

3 Edit and click anywhere off the object to close the application.

❑ **Edit in the application**

4 Right-click to open the short menu and choose Object > Open.

5 Edit, and use the application's File > Close and Return… to exit.

Working simply within the host application, you can change the size and position of an embedded object. If you want to edit or reformat its contents, you must use its original application. You can do this at two levels:

● run a limited version, within the host application;

  or

● open the full version of the original application and work on the object there.

Tip

If you are importing an Excel chart, the Picture format takes least space, but you must use the Excel Chart format if you want to be able to edit it.

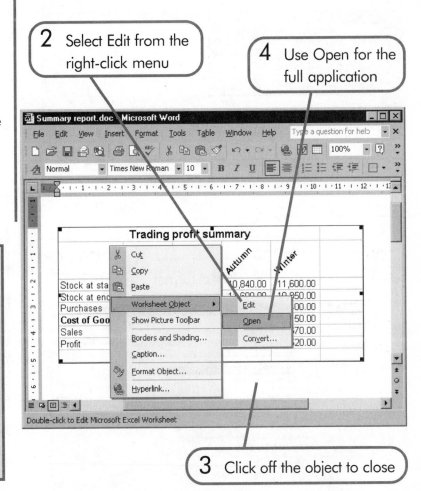

2 Select Edit from the right-click menu

4 Use Open for the full application

3 Click off the object to close

Linking

The one crucial difference between embedding and linking is that with a linked object, there is only one set of data. When you edit the original file – the source data – the contents of the linked object are changed to match.

1   Copy the block of text or object to be linked.

2   In the host document, open the Edit menu and select Paste Special.

3   Select Paste Link.

4   If you have a choice of As formats, select the most suitable one for the job.

5   Click [OK].

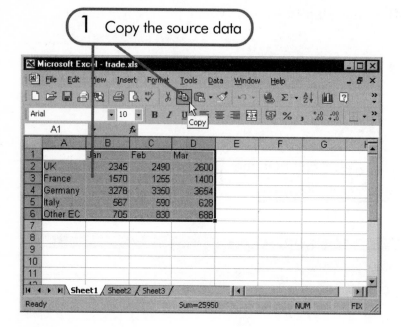

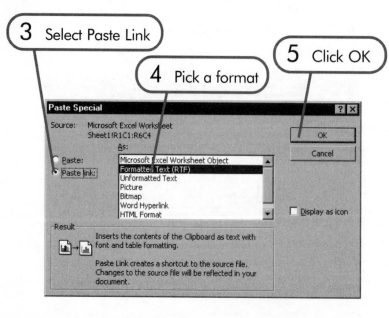

Tip

The type of data that is being linked in determines the choice of Paste Special formats. When in doubt, use the Object format.

140

Editing linked objects

Take note

When you open the source application to edit a linked object, the changes are made to the source file.

All linked objects can be edited by double-clicking on them to call up their original application. Those pasted in the Object format can only be edited this way.

In Object, Picture or Bitmap format, you can alter the size and position of the linked object.

With Formatted or Plain Text, you can also edit them using the host application's tools – though these edits will only last until the link is updated. This is only worth doing if you want to prettify something for immediate printing.

The month names have been edited to appear in full in this linked object. (Compare them with the Excel table opposite.) However, as soon as that Excel file is edited, or when the file is next opened, the link will be updated and the original headings restored.

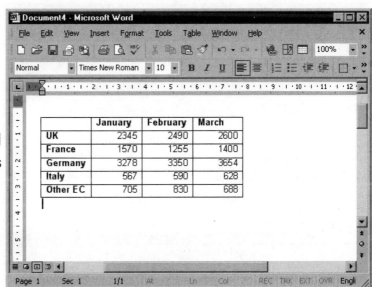

	January	February	March
UK	2345	2490	2600
France	1570	1255	1400
Germany	3278	3350	3654
Italy	567	590	628
Other EC	705	830	688

Tip

When you open a document that contains linked objects, the source files are checked to update the objects. It therefore takes longer to open the document. For best performance, only link when it is really necessary.

The Office Clipboard

When you cut or copy data into the Windows Clipboard, it replaces whatever was there previously. This is not true with Office XP, where the Clipboard can hold up to 24 items. As these can be pasted individually or all at once, it can be very useful for reorganising documents and for collating data from a variety of sources.

● When you do a **Paste All**, the items are pasted in the order in which they were copied.

● Individual items can be deleted from the Clipboard.

Basic steps

1 The Clipboard should be open in the Task Pane. If it isn't, use Edit > Office Clipboard to display it.

2 Move within or between applications, copying items in the order that you want them to appear.

3 Move to where you want to paste and click on a single item or click ⧉ Paste All to place all the items at once.

4 To empty the Clipboard, click ⧉ Clear All .

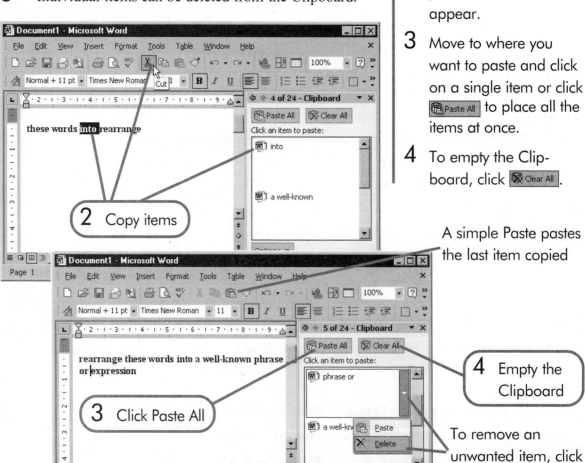

2 Copy items

A simple Paste pastes the last item copied

3 Click Paste All

4 Empty the Clipboard

To remove an unwanted item, click on the arrow bar and select Delete

Inserted objects

Complete files can be linked into documents using the **Insert Object** command. Though the whole file is linked, not all of it will be displayed – you will see part of a Word or Excel document, or the first slide of a presentation. If you edit it, you can access the rest, or scroll to a different part of the document to change the visible area.

Inserted file objects can be:

- created at the time, from within the host document, or loaded in from file;

- either embedded or linked;

- displayed normally or present just as icons. In either case, the Edit and Open options for the source application are on the short menu.

The menus that you get when you right-click on an object depend mainly on the application, though the Object sub-menus vary with the nature of the object.

Word object (in Excel)

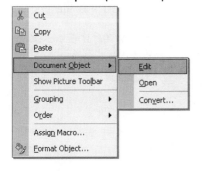

Excel object (in PowerPoint)

PowerPoint object (in Word)

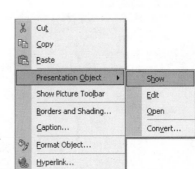

With a linked object, Edit and Open both call up the full application. If the object is not linked, Edit gives you the limited version of the application, within the host document.

Inserting an object

Once you have decided what you want to insert, and whether to place it as an icon or displayed object, the insertion is easy.

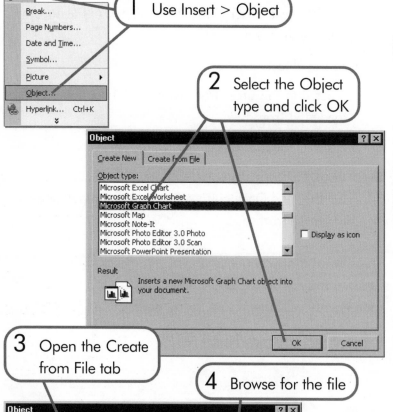

1 Use Insert > Object

2 Select the Object type and click OK

3 Open the Create from File tab

4 Browse for the file

5 Link or embed?

6 Click OK

Basic steps

1 Open the Insert menu and select Object.

❑ Creating a new file

2 On the Create New tab, select the Object type and click OK. The application will open within the document.

❑ Using an existing file

3 Open the Create from File tab.

4 Click ☐ Browse... ☐ to locate the file.

5 Turn on Link to file, if wanted, or leave it off to embed the file.

6 If you want the file as a visible object, click ☐ OK ☐.

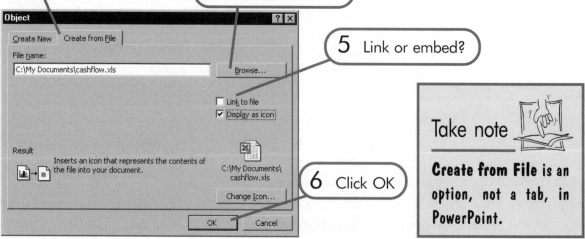

Take note

Create from File is an option, not a tab, in **PowerPoint**.

Basic steps

1 Follow steps opposite to to select the Object type or file.

2 Turn on the Display as Icon option.

3 Click [Change Icon...].

4 Check out icons in the list to see if there is one you prefer.

5 Replace the filename with a brief Caption.

6 Click [OK].

Icons for links

If you want your readers to open (or run) the linked file to see it properly, it may be better to place it as an icon. Most computer users nowadays need little prompting to click an icon, though they may well need prompting to click on a spreadsheet table, block of text or other image.

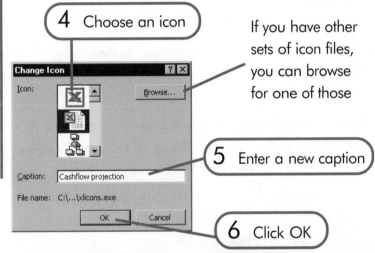

4 Choose an icon

If you have other sets of icon files, you can browse for one of those

5 Enter a new caption

6 Click OK

Tip

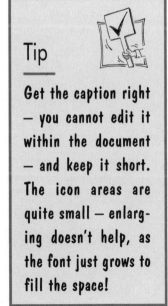

Get the caption right — you cannot edit it within the document — and keep it short. The icon areas are quite small — enlarging doesn't help, as the font just grows to fill the space!

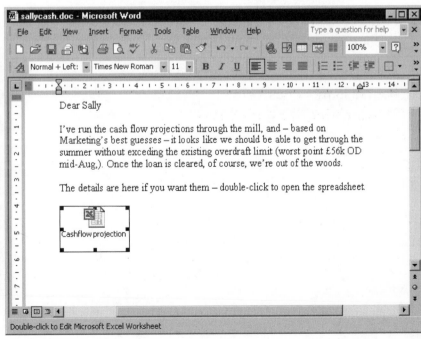

Dear Sally

I've run the cash flow projections through the mill, and – based on Marketing's best guesses – it looks like we should be able to get through the summer without exceeding the existing overdraft limit (worst point £56k OD mid-Aug,). Once the loan is cleared, of course, we're out of the woods.

The details are here if you want them – double-click to open the spreadsheet

Cashflow projection

Summary

- ❏ The Edit > Copy and Paste commands can be used to copy data from one application to another. Depending upon the type of data and the applications, the copy may become an integral part of the target document, or may be embedded in it.

- ❏ Embedded objects can be edited by calling up their original application from within their new document.

- ❏ Linked objects retain the connection to their original file. If this is edited, the changes will be seen in the new document.

- ❏ Data can be pasted or paste linked into a document, in a variety of formats. The choice of formats depends upon the type of data and the source application.

- ❏ The Office Clipboard can hold up to 24 separate blocks of copied data. They can be pasted individually or all at once – in their stored order.

- ❏ Files from different applications can be included in documents as Inserted objects.

- ❏ Linked and Inserted objects can be displayed in their normal format or as icons.

9 Outlook

Getting organised

Outlook is a personal organiser, and if you are on a network, it can also be used for arranging meetings of group members.

This is a multi-function system, with its various parts accessed through the **Outlook Bar** down the left side. When you select an item from here, it is displayed in the main window.

The bar has three groups.

Outlook Shortcuts

- **Outlook Today**, a summary of your appointments, current tasks and e-mail waiting for processing;

- **Inbox**, containing you new mail messages – and old ones that have not yet been deleted or filed elsewhere!

- A **Calendar**, with a reminder facility (page 152);

- A list of **Contact** names, addresses, phone and fax numbers, with a built-in phone dialler (page 150);

- A **Tasks** list, for scheduling tasks and monitoring their progress (page 158);

- A **Journal** for recording work and time spent (page 160).

- **Notes** for jotting down reminders to yourself – these can be stuck anywhere on the desktop (page 162).

The elements can be interrelated, linking tasks to contacts or meetings, and contacts to meetings.

My Shortcuts

These links are to the less-used folders and facilities:

- **Drafts**, where messages can be held before completion;

- **Outbox**, where message sit while waiting for delivery;

- **Sent**, where copies of your messages are kept;

Take note

If you like, you can run your working sessions entirely from within Outlook – you can reach your files, programs and every other part of your system from here.

Take note

If you have been using the earlier version of Outlook in Office 97 or 2000, the contacts lists and other data will be copied into Outlook when it is first set up.

The display varies with the element being used, and has special options for each type. This screenshot is from Calendar in a Week view, set here to show a 7-day diary, the month and the Task list.

- **Outlook Update**, which links to Microsoft's on-line update service;
- **Journal** for logging activites.

Other Shortcuts

These provides access to regularly-used folders. You will find links to *My Computer*, and to the *My Documents* and *Favorites* folders. Files can be managed here, just as in Explorer – use it to open, view, print, rename, or send them to another disk or through the mail. You can even run programs from here!

Click to open the function

This deletes any selected item

Display options

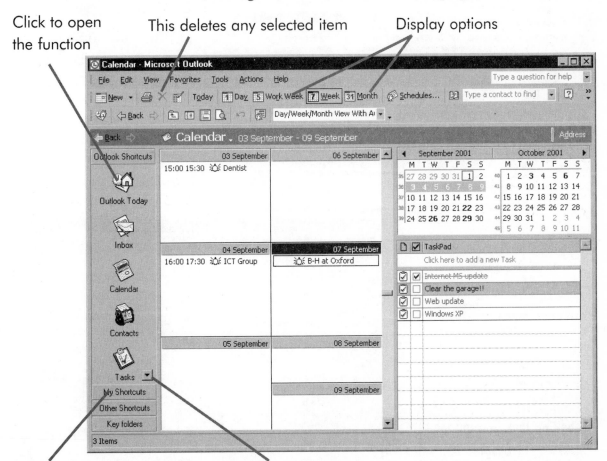

Click to open up the group

Scroll to reach other items in the group

The Contacts list

This is probably the most straightforward part of Outlook to set up. Mind you, it will take a while if you give all the details that it can hold – home and business address, phone and fax, birthdays, spouse, assistant, dog's name…

Basic steps

1 Open Contacts.

2 Open the New menu and select Contact or click ⊂≡ New ▾ .

3 On the General tab, enter the name and other contact details.

4 Switch to other tabs to add more if wanted.

5 Click 💾 Save and Close .

❑ The new name will be slotted into the list in alphabetical order

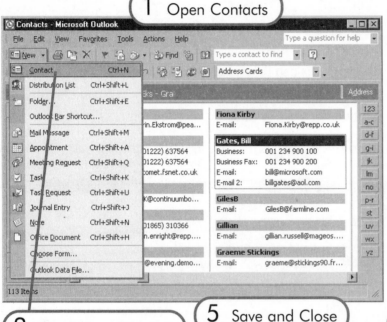

1 Open Contacts

2 Use New > Contact

Take note

We'll get back to e-mail when we look 'Beyond the desktop' in Chapter 10.

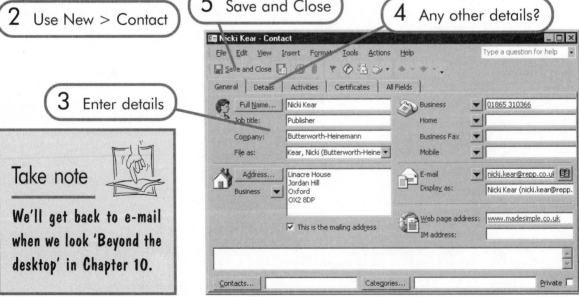

5 Save and Close

4 Any other details?

3 Enter details

Basic steps

1 Open Contacts.

2 Use the index buttons, if necessary, to get to the right place.

3 Select the person.

4 Click 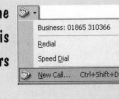 or select Call Contact from the Actions menu.

5 Click Start Call.

6 Lift the phone.

7 When you want to hang up, click End Call.

Phone dialling

If your phone is connected through the PC's modem, you can get Outlook to dial for you.

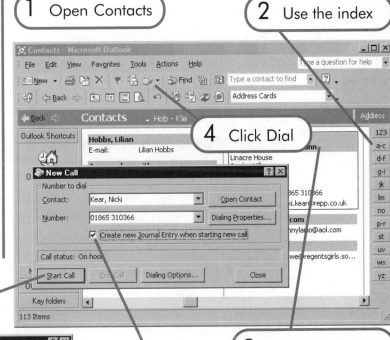

1 Open Contacts

2 Use the index

4 Click Dial

5 Start the call

3 Select the contact

Do you want to log the call? (See page 160.)

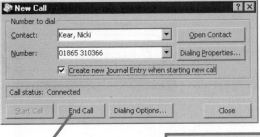

7 Click End Call

Take note

The dialler's drop-down list lets you repeat the last call, make a New Call to a number that is not in your book, Redial recently used numbers or access your Speed Dial list.

Business: 01865 310366
Redial
Speed Dial
New Call... Ctrl+Shift+D

Calendar options

Many of the Outlook options can be left at their defaults; some should be looked at when you have got used to Outlook and want to fine-tune it; the Calendar needs early attention. You need to set the defaults for:

● How long before a meeting you receive a reminder;

● The pattern of your working week, and working day;

● The public holidays for your country.

1 Open Tools menu and select Options...

2 On the Preferences tab, set the length of the Reminder notice.

3 Click Calendar Options... .

4 Tick your working days.

5 Set your normal working hours.

6 Click Add Holidays... .

7 Select the countries.

8 Click OK then close the Options window.

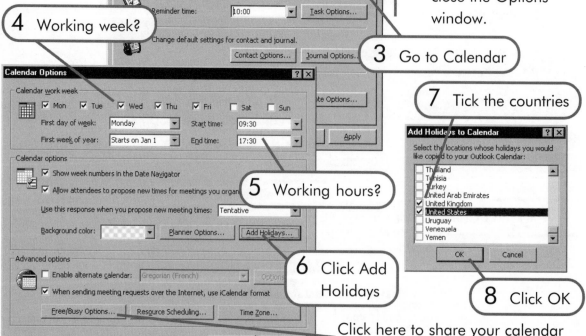

2 Set the Reminder notice

4 Working week?

3 Go to Calendar

7 Tick the countries

5 Working hours?

6 Click Add Holidays

8 Click OK

Click here to share your calendar bookings with networked colleagues

Basic steps

1 Open the Calendar.

2 Switch to 1 Day view.

3 Select the day.

4 Point to the start time and drag the highlight to the planned end time.

5 Click ⬛New ▾ or select Appointment from the New menu.

6 Enter a Subject.

7 Enter the Location.

8 Click 🖫 Save and Close.

Making a date

A simple appointment can be set up in seconds.

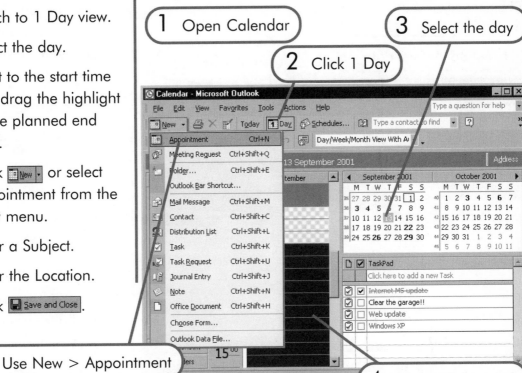

1 Open Calendar

2 Click 1 Day

3 Select the day

5 Use New > Appointment

4 Highlight the times

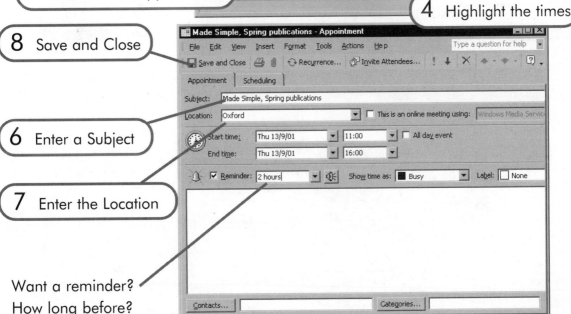

8 Save and Close

6 Enter a Subject

7 Enter the Location

Want a reminder? How long before?

153

Recurring appointments

If you have a series of regular appointments, you can set them all up in one operation.

1 Set up the first date

2 Click Recurrence

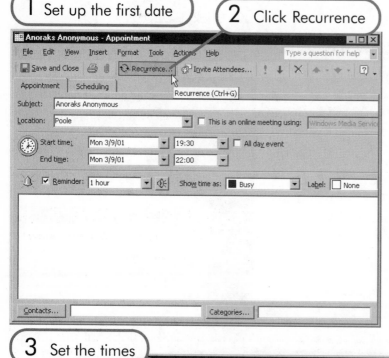

3 Set the times

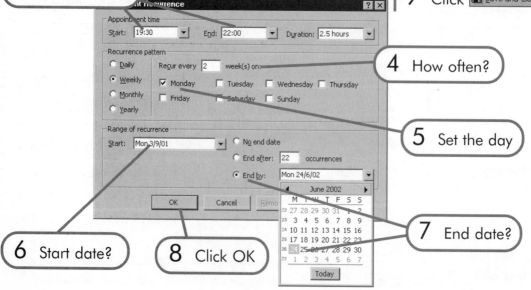

4 How often?

5 Set the day

6 Start date?

8 Click OK

7 End date?

1. Follow steps 1 to 7 on the previous page to set the day and time of the first appointment of the series.

2. Click ⟲ Recurrence... .

3. Check the times.

4. In Recurrence pattern, set the frequency.

5. Set the Day (of the week, month or year).

6. Check the Start date.

7. Select No end date, or End after or End by and set the limit.

8. Click OK .

9. Click 💾 Save and Close .

Arranging meetings

1 Select the day and
time as for an ap-
pointment (see page
153).

2 Select New > Meeting
Request from the
Calendar menu.

3 Click the To: button.

...cont

This is probably of most use to people working on a local area
network, where each has access to the (public) diary of the
others. But, it is also a convenient way to call a meeting with
those whom you can contact by fax or e-mail.

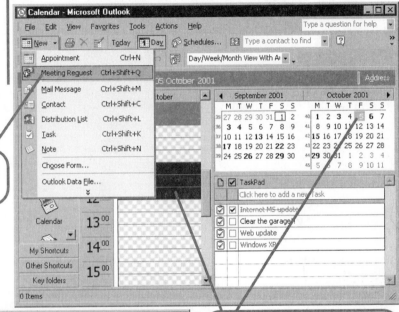

2 Use New > Meeting
Request

3 Click To:

1 Set the date and time

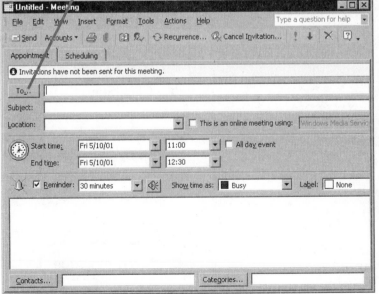

Take note

When you have finished arranging the meeting, Outlook
will send faxes and e-mails
containing the details and
notes you have typed into the
Appointment panel.

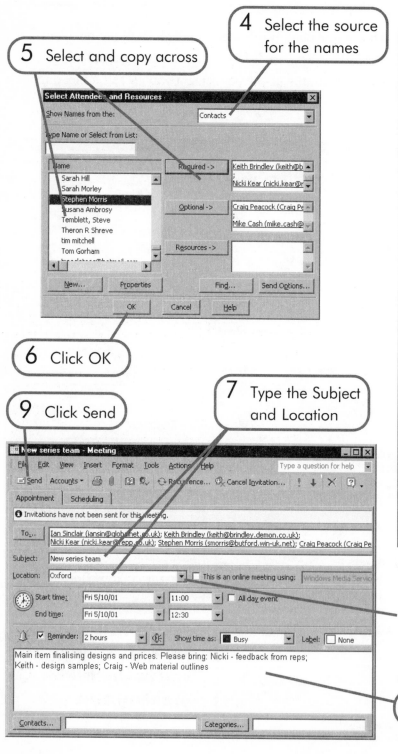

5 Select and copy across

4 Select the source for the names

6 Click OK

9 Click Send

7 Type the Subject and Location

8 Add a message

cont…

4 Select the source for the names – probably Post Office Address book for the local area network and Contacts for external mail and fax.

5 Select the attendees who are Required or Optional, or will supply Resources, and click the buttons to copy them to the appropriate panes.

6 Click [OK].

7 Back at the Appointment panel, type the Subject and Location.

8 Type any message that you want to add to the meeting notice.

9 Click Send.

Previously-used locations can be picked from the drop-down list

Basic steps

1 If you have closed the Appointment window, double-click on the time to re-open it.

2 Go to the Scheduling tab.

3 Check for clashes – you can only do this for people on your local network.

❑ To adjust the time

4 Drag the start or end line for minor adjustments.

Or

5 Click `<< AutoPick Next >>` heading backwards and forwards to let Outlook find the next free time for all attendees.

6 Type a message on the Appointments panel, if needed.

7 Click the Send button, or if you have already sent a request, click the Send Update button.

Checking availability

Where the other attendees are on your local area network – and are all using Outlook's Calendar to plan their time – you can check their availability. On the Attendee Availability tab, you can see who is busy when, and can rearrange your meeting time if necessary.

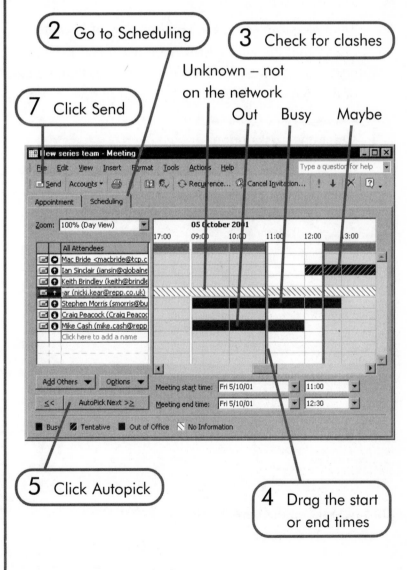

2 Go to Scheduling

3 Check for clashes

7 Click Send

Unknown – not on the network

Out   Busy   Maybe

5 Click Autopick

4 Drag the start or end times

Tasks

Use the Tasks module to keep track of your current and scheduled tasks. For each task you can record:

● The start and due dates;

● The percentage complete;

● The status and priority;

● The *Categories* – this can be just a way of keeping the same kinds of jobs together, or it can be a way of organising multi-part projects and monitoring the progress of the component tasks.

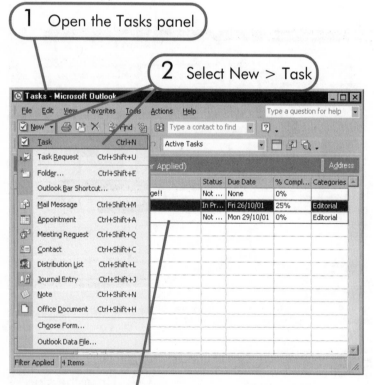

1 Open the Tasks panel

2 Select New > Task

Just type a Subject here to set up a new Task quickly

Completed tasks are crossed off – use ☒ to delete them when the records are no longer needed

1 Open the Tasks panel.

2 Drop down the New list and select Task or click ☑ New ▾.

3 Type a Subject.

4 Set the Due date and Start date, if relevant.

5 Select the Status from the drop-down list.

6 Click Categories... .

7 Select one or more Categories.

8 Click OK .

9 Switch to the Details tab and add any known details.

10 Click 🖫 Save and Close .

Take note

If you don't want to enter the details for a new task, type the Subject into the 'Click here to add a new task' slot. Double-click to open the Task panel, and add or edit the details later.

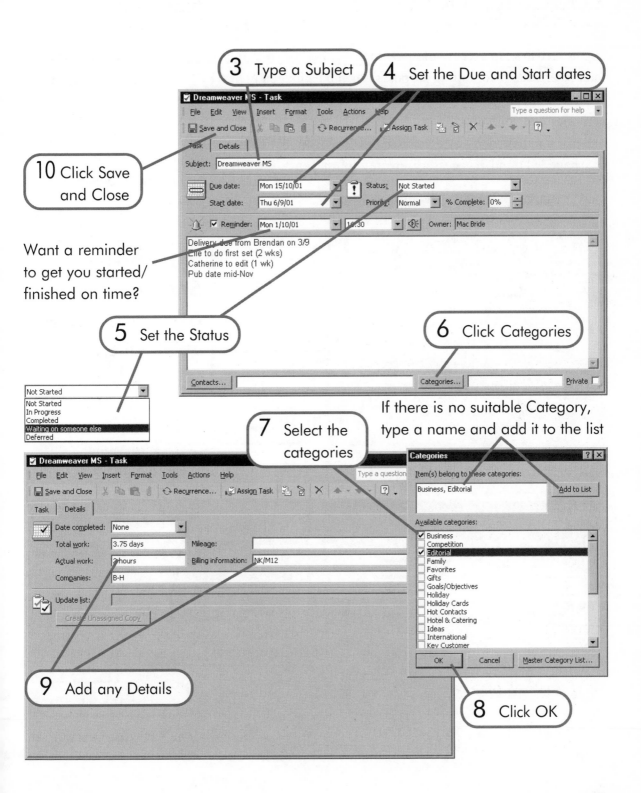

3 Type a Subject

4 Set the Due and Start dates

10 Click Save and Close

Want a reminder to get you started/ finished on time?

5 Set the Status

6 Click Categories

If there is no suitable Category, type a name and add it to the list

7 Select the categories

9 Add any Details

8 Click OK

Logging activities

If you need to keep a record of work done – either for your own later reference, or for billing purposes – it can be logged in the Journal. The simplest way to do this is to get Outlook to log the activities that you normally need to record – unwanted entries are easily removed. You can also log calls as you make them (see page 151), and, if necessary, create a Journal entry directly.

(see page 151)

Basic steps

1 Open the Tools menu and select Options.

2 Click ☐ Journal Options... .

3 Tick the items, files and contacts you want to log and click OK.

❑ Single entry

4 Open the Journal panel and click 🖉 New ▾.

5 Type the Subject.

6 Note the time spent.

7 Select a Category.

8 Click 🖫 Save and Close .

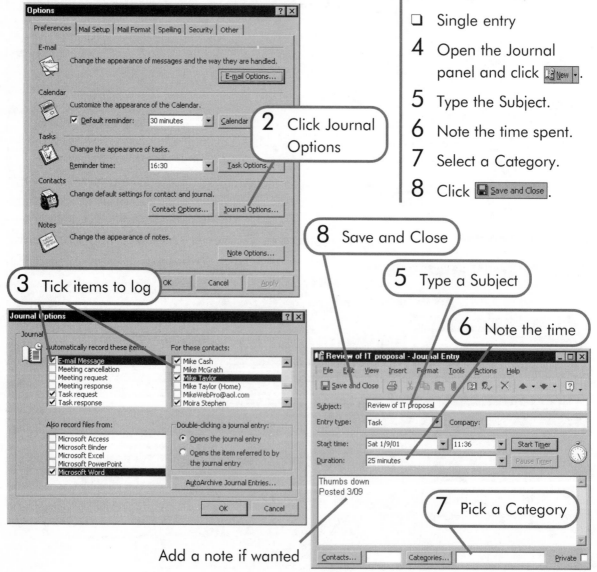

2 Click Journal Options

8 Save and Close

5 Type a Subject

3 Tick items to log

6 Note the time

7 Pick a Category

Add a note if wanted

160

Viewing activities

❑ Using the Journal

1 Open the Journal.

2 Select a View – the *Last Seven Days* view is probably the best.

3 Right-click on an entry for the short menu.

4 Select Open Journal Entry to edit the entry.

5 Select Open Item Referred To to open logged files in their applications.

❑ Contact Activities

6 Go to Contacts and select the person.

7 Switch to the Activities tab.

8 Select the type of items from the Show list.

If you want to view all your logged activities, the Journal panel is the place to do it. However, it may often be more useful to view the activities in relation to a contact, and this is best done through the Contacts panel.

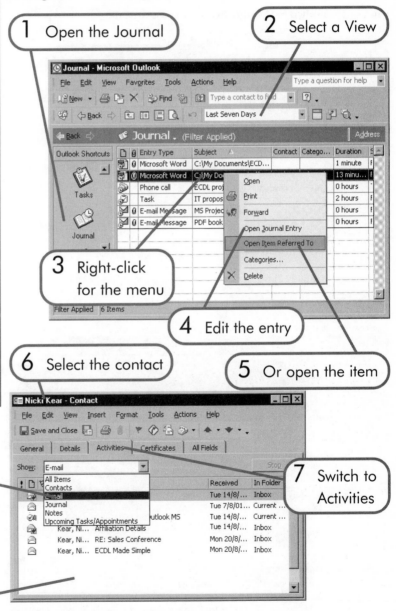

1 Open the Journal

2 Select a View

3 Right-click for the menu

4 Edit the entry

6 Select the contact

5 Or open the item

8 Select the items to show

7 Switch to Activities

All relevant items are listed, not just the logged ones – to see just those, select Journal in the Show list

Notes

If you are the sort of person who writes notes to yourself, here is an alternative to having Post-Its™ stuck to the side of your monitor. Outlook Notes save paper, and they don't drop off! You can keep them in the Notes folder, or stick them anywhere on your desktop – though not onto documents.

Basic steps

1 Open the Notes panel.

2 Open the New menu and select Note or click ⊕ New ▾.

3 Type your note – if you put a title in the top line, it will stand out more in the folder.

4 Drag the note onto the desktop, if wanted.

5 Click   to close the note – it will be saved.

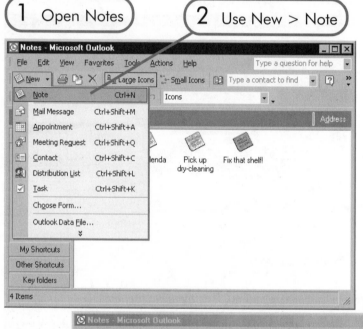

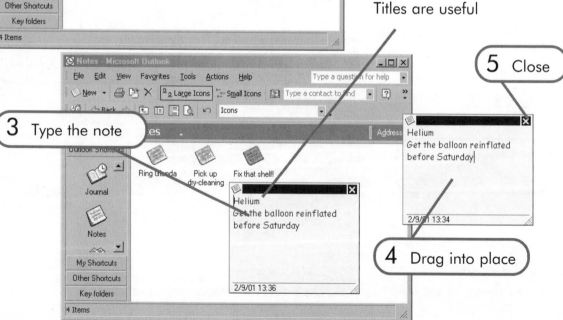

162

Reminders

Tip

Set the time of day for your Task reminders in the Tools > Options Preferences panel. (The Task Options just set the colours for Overdue and Completed tasks.)

We have seen that you can set reminders for appointments and tasks. Those for appointments appear 15 minutes (or however long you chose) before the event; reminders for tasks appear at a set time. The default reminder time for tasks is typically the start of the day.

When the Reminders dialog box appears it offers three options:

● Click **Dismiss** to clear the reminder (or **Dismiss All** if there are several on the same box);

● Set the delay and click **Snooze** for another reminder some time later;

● Use **Open Item** to read the event or task panel.

When do you want
Task reminders?

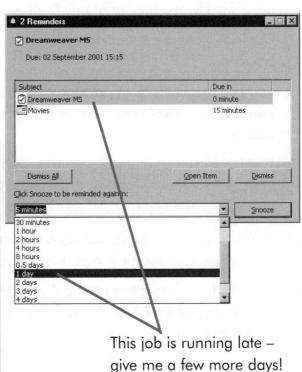

This job is running late –
give me a few more days!

Summary

- Outlook is a personal and workgroup organiser in which you can store contacts, appointments and lists of tasks.

- The Contacts list can be used to record very complete details of your contacts.

- You can dial phone numbers in your Contacts list by clicking the dialler button.

- Most of the Options can be left at their defaults, but you should set up the Calendar options, and the Reminder notice time.

- When adding appointments, you can set them to recur weekly, monthly or at any fixed interval.

- Reminders can be set for any time before an appointment.

- You can use Outlook to arrange meetings with other users on your local area network, or who are accessible by e-mail or fax.

- The Task list can be used to schedule activities and to record progress on them. Reminders can be set for time-limited tasks.

- The Journal can log your activities automatically, and entries can also be made at any time.

- You need never forget anything if you set Reminders for your appointments and tasks, and stick Notes about other things on your Desktop.

10 Beyond the desktop

Internet links

In the Microsoft vision of the future, the world is your desktop. They see a time when the Internet will be as accessible as your local area network, and you will exchange ideas and documents as easily with colleagues around the world as you do now with those in your office.

In newer versions of Windows, *Windows Explorer* and *Internet Explorer* are fully interchangeable. They may look different when you first run them, but that is only because of the way you have used them – open the Folders in Internet Explorer's sidebar, and it turns into Windows Explorer; type an Internet URL into the address line of Windows Explorer and it turns into Internet Explorer! You can use either to access the files on your hard disks, the other computers on your local network, the pages of the World Wide Web and everything else that is on-line.

Office XP likewise has Web browsing and e-mail facilities in all its applications, and links to Internet resources at key points (see opposite).

The Web toolbar will be familiar to anyone who has used Internet Explorer.

Tip

If you have Internet Explorer or any other Web browser on your system, this will be activated when you try to go anywhere using the Web toolbar in an Office application. You can stop this by going to Windows Explorer and removing or redefining the HTM and HTML File Types. I wouldn't bother. The browser will load up in a few seconds, and it will do a better job than the application.

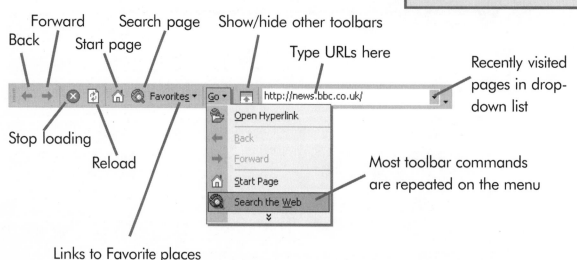

Back

Forward

Start page

Search page

Show/hide other toolbars

Type URLs here

Recently visited pages in drop-down list

Stop loading

Reload

Links to Favorite places

Most toolbar commands are repeated on the menu

Clip art offers a good example of the 'world-is-your-desktop' approach – and of its limitations.

Click 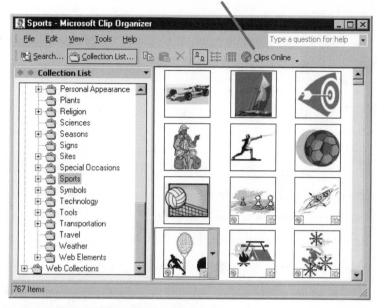 Clips Online in the Clip Organizer to go to Microsoft's Design Gallery on the Web. There must be thousands of files there, available to licensed Office users without charge.

If you have a fast ISDN or broadband connection to the Internet, you will get there quickly. If the Microsoft site, and the connections along the route,

Go to the Design Gallery online

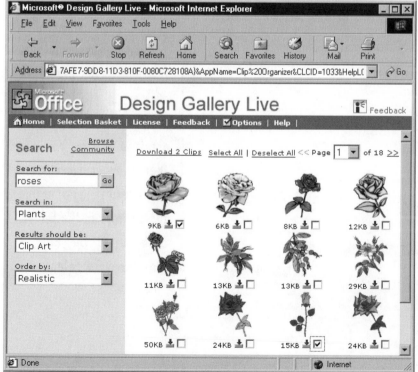

are not too busy, you will be able to find and download files quickly, but if you have a dial-up connection, and the site or the Internet's lines are busy, you can wait ages for your files.

The world's telephone connections and the Internet's hardware need a lot more development before we can all treat the Internet as an extension of our desktops.

Outlook Inbox

Outlook's mail system is organised through four folders:

- **Inbox**, where incoming mail is stored. Messages remain in here until you delete them or move them elsewhere.

- **Drafts**, where part-written messages can be saved. Use the File > Save command while working on a message, and it will be saved in this folder. You can later reopen it, finish it and send as normal.

- **Outbox**, where messages sit while awaiting delivery;

- **Sent Items**, which stores copies of all outgoing mail. If not wanted, you can turn off the automatic copying in the e-mail options of the Tools > Options > Preferences panel.

The Inbox is the one you will use most often, and is on the Outlook bar. If you are on a network with a permanent connection to the Internet, all your new mail will probably be sent directly to it. If not, you'll have to pick up the mail for yourself.

- If you normally perform Send/Receive manually, go to the Mail Setup tab of the Options dialog box and turn on **Hang up when finished**.

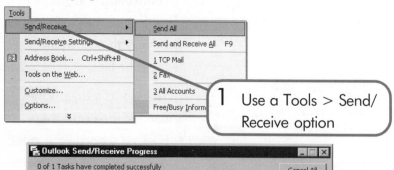

1 Use a Tools > Send/ Receive option

3 Wait while messages are transferred

Basic steps

- ❑ Getting the mail

1 Click ⊞ Send/Receive or open the Tools menu, point to Send/Receive and select your mail service.

2 If you are not on-line, Outlook will start up the connection.

3 Wait while Outlook sends and downloads new messages.

Tip

You can create new folders for long-term organised storage, if required. Use File > New > Folder to create a folder. You can then copy or move messages into it, by dragging them across to the folder, or by using the Edit > Move/Copy To Folder.

Basic steps

❑ Reading and replying

1 Click on a message, or right-click and select Open.

2 Read the message.

3 Use the buttons or the Actions menu, and select Reply, or Reply to All (send to all who received a copy), or Forward (send a copy to another person).

4 Select Plain Text or HTML format.

5 Continue as for sending mail (next page).

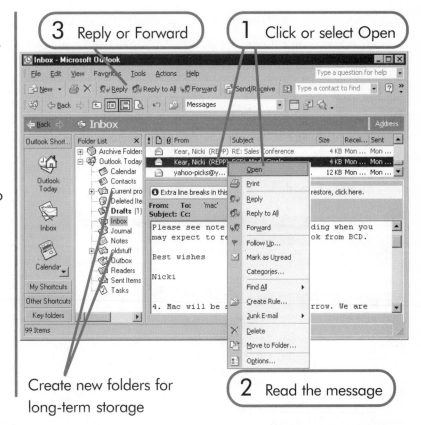

3 Reply or Forward

1 Click or select Open

Create new folders for long-term storage

2 Read the message

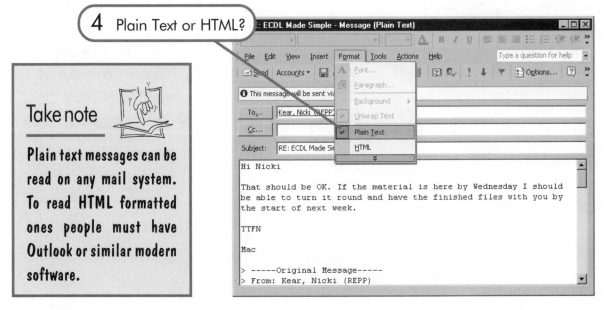

4 Plain Text or HTML?

Take note

Plain text messages can be read on any mail system. To read HTML formatted ones people must have Outlook or similar modern software.

Sending e-mail

E-mail has transformed business and personal communications. It is cheap, fast and reliable – and if a message does not get through, your mail server will let you know. But it does need to be used with a bit of thought.

● Type a clear **Subject** line, so your recipients know that your message is not junk e-mail to be ignored;

● Keep messages short – people may have to pay for phone time to download them.

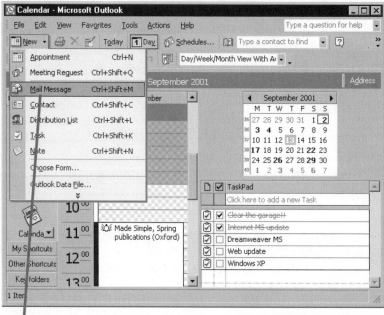

1   Use New >
       Mail Message

You can start a new message from any part of Outlook.

Basic steps

1 In any part of Outlook select Mail Message from the New... menu.

Or

2 In Inbox or any mail folder, click 🗐 New ▾.

3 At the new message window, click To...

4 Select the recipient and click To -> or Cc -> for copies – repeat if needed.

5 Click OK.

6 Type a Subject, then your message.

7 Click 🗄 Options... to open the Options panel.

8 Set the Sensitivity, Delivery time and other options as required and click Close.

9 Click ✉ Send.

Take note

If an address is not in your Contacts, you can add it at step 4.

170

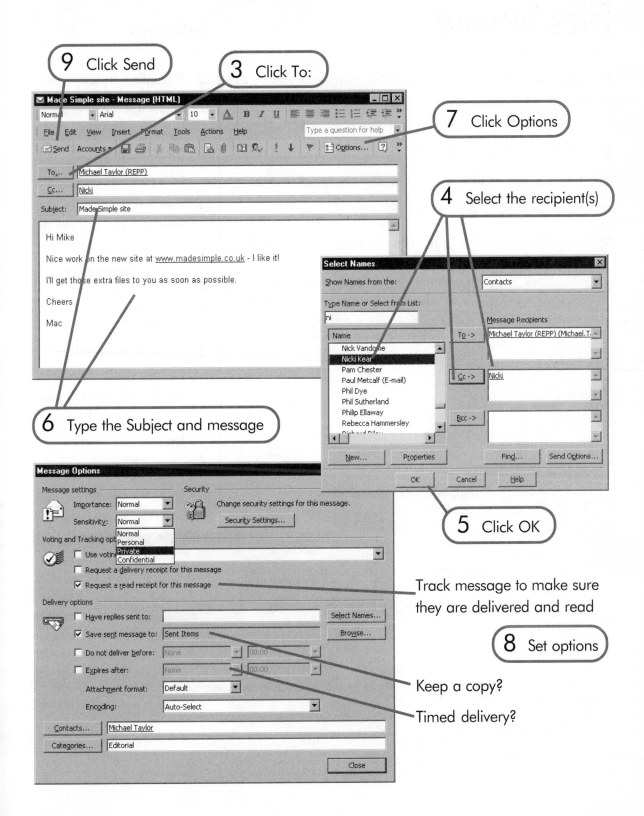

9 Click Send

3 Click To:

7 Click Options

4 Select the recipient(s)

6 Type the Subject and message

5 Click OK

Track message to make sure they are delivered and read

8 Set options

Keep a copy?

Timed delivery?

Made Simple site - Message (HTML)

Normal | Arial | 10 | A | B | I | U

File Edit View Insert Format Tools Actions Help

Type a question for help

Send Accounts Options...

To... | Michael Taylor (REPP)

Cc... | Nicki

Subject: | Made Simple site

Hi Mike

Nice work on the new site at www.madesimple.co.uk - I like it!

I'll get those extra files to you as soon as possible.

Cheers

Mac

Select Names

Show Names from the: | Contacts

Type Name or Select from List:

ni

Name

Nick Vandome
Nicki Kear
Pam Chester
Paul Metcalf (E-mail)
Phil Dye
Phil Sutherland
Philip Ellaway
Rebecca Hammersley
Richard Riley

To -> | Michael Taylor (REPP) (Michael.T.

Message Recipients

Cc -> | Nicki

Bcc ->

New... Properties Find... Send Options...

OK Cancel Help

Message Options

Message settings

Importance: | Normal
Sensitivity: | Normal

Security

Change security settings for this message.

Security Settings...

Voting and Tracking opt

Normal
Personal
Private
Confidential

Use voting

Request a delivery receipt for this message

Request a read receipt for this message

Delivery options

Have replies sent to: | | Select Names...

Save sent message to: | Sent Items | Browse...

Do not deliver before: | None | 00:00

Expires after: | None | 00:00

Attachment format: | Default

Encoding: | Auto-Select

Contacts... | Michael Taylor

Categories... | Editorial

Close

Files by wire

Experts have been telling us for years that computers will create the paperless office, but in most offices so far they seem to have created even more paper. Office can help to reverse that!

● Send e-mail documents, from within an application.

● Attach documents to e-mail messages as you write them.

● Circulate documents, by adding a Routing slip.

● Send faxes directly from your PC, without printing first.

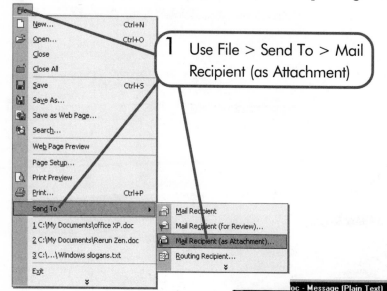

1 Use File > Send To > Mail Recipient (as Attachment)

❑ E-mailing documents

1 From the File menu, select Send To then Mail Recipient (as Attachment)...

❑ The new message window opens, with the document embedded in the message area.

2 Click [To...] and select the recipient(s).

3 If the document has been given a Title, it will be copied into the Subject line – if not, type a header here.

4 Add a message and send as usual.

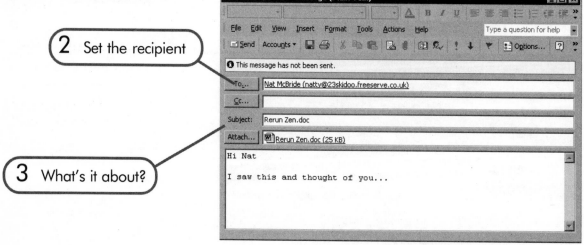

2 Set the recipient

3 What's it about?

Basic steps

1 From the File menu, select Send To then Routing Recipient...

2 Click [Address...] and select the recipients.

3 Click [Route] to circulate the document immediately.

or

4 Click [Add Slip] to leave it set for later routing.

Tip

Send To > Mail Recipient adds e-mail facilities to Word so that you can send the document as a message. Click 📧 on the standard Toolbar to revert to the normal Word screen.

Routing slips

If you want several people to see and make comments on a draft document, you can circulate it around the internal network, or through your Internet connections, by adding a Routing slip. You can control the order in which the document is circulated, and also what can be done to it.

● Use **Tracked changes** to turn on revision marking, so that you can see what changes have been made;

● Use **Comments**, to allow others to add notes, but not change the document;

● The **Forms** option is only for circulating forms for collecting information.

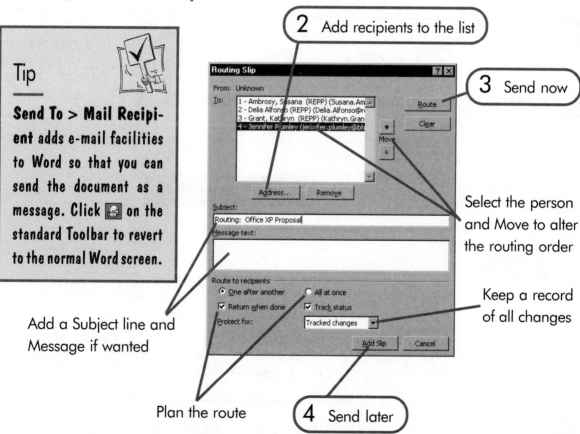

2 Add recipients to the list

3 Send now

Select the person and Move to alter the routing order

Keep a record of all changes

Add a Subject line and Message if wanted

Plan the route

4 Send later

❑ Sending faxes

1 From the File menu, select Send then Fax Recipient... to start the Fax Wizard.

2 The first time, work through the stages, clicking Next.

or

3 On later uses, skip to those stages that need new settings.

4 If there is a Cover page, add your details.

5 Click Send Fax Now.

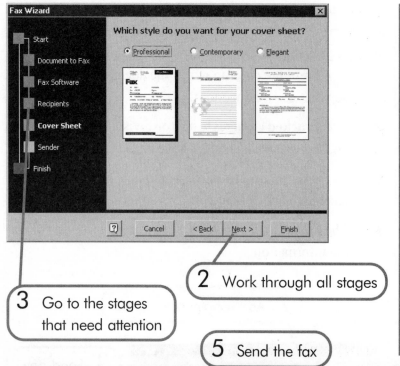

2 Work through all stages

3 Go to the stages that need attention

5 Send the fax

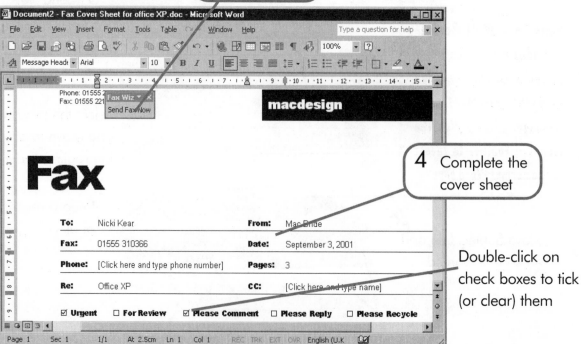

4 Complete the cover sheet

Double-click on check boxes to tick (or clear) them

Basic steps

❏ Attaching files

1 Start to write a new message .

2 Open the Insert menu, select File or click [📎].

3 Type the Filename or browse for the file.

4 Click [Insert ▾].

5 Complete and send the message as usual.

Tip

Sometimes a hyperlink will do the job better than inserting the file. See the next page.

Attached files

Any files – from any application, not just Office 2000 – can be attached or linked to an e-mail. Use a Link if the recipient is on your local network, and the document file is in a public folder – it is more efficient that actually sending the file.

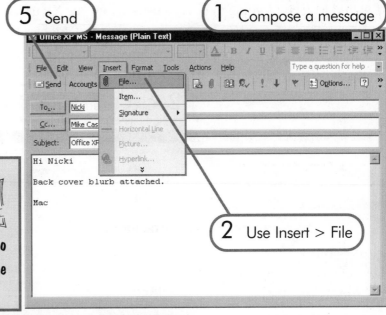

5 Send

1 Compose a message

2 Use Insert > File

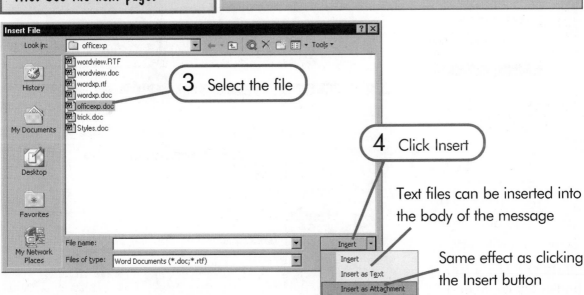

3 Select the file

4 Click Insert

Text files can be inserted into the body of the message

Same effect as clicking the Insert button

Hyperlinks

A hyperlink can take you from one file to another on the same computer or on a totally different system on the other side of the world. All Office XP applications can handle hyperlinks. You can create them and travel along them in e-mail messages, Word reports, spreadsheets or databases.

If your document is going to be read by other Office XP users, and you want to draw their attention to a file on a public folder in your computer or network, or on the Internet, don't embed it or attach it – use a hyperlink.

Basic steps

❑ Creating a hyperlink

1 Select the word or phrase (or picture).

2 Use Insert > Hyperlink or click 🖭 .

3 Type or select the Internet address or the file to be linked.

4 Click [OK].

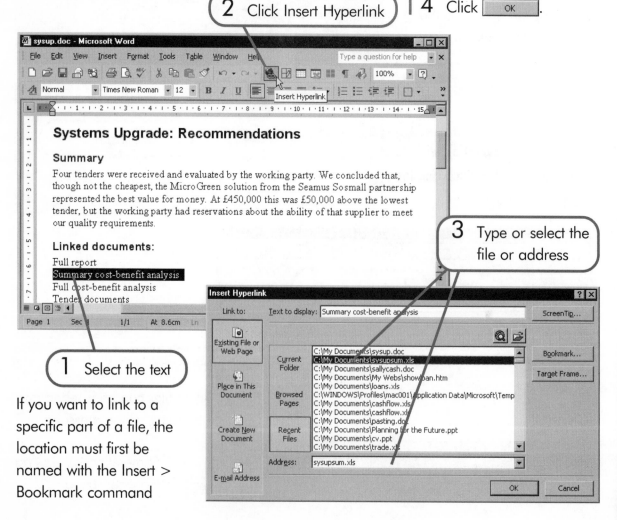

2 Click Insert Hyperlink

3 Type or select the file or address

1 Select the text

If you want to link to a specific part of a file, the location must first be named with the Insert > Bookmark command

Basic steps

❑ Using hyperlinks

1 Point to underlined text, hold down [Control] and click.

2 Wait for the linked document (and its application) to load.

3 The Web toolbar will have appeared. Use its Back and Forwards buttons to navigate between the linked documents.

If you pause over a link, its URL will appear; hold down [Control] and the pointer becomes a hand – click to follow the link

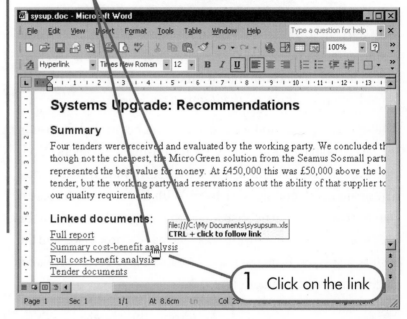

1 Click on the link

3 Move between the linked files

2 Wait while it loads

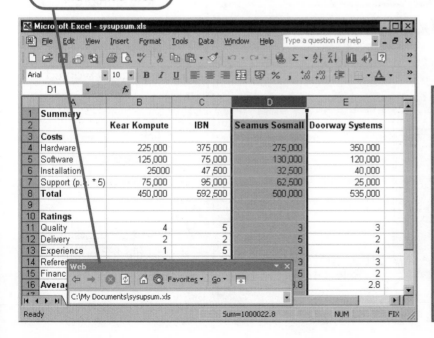

Tip

If you want to create a Web site, FrontPage is an ideal tool for the job. Read *FrontPage 2000 Made Simple* to find out more about it.

HTML

All Office XP documents can be saved in Web page (.HTM) format. This doesn't mean that you can save a file as HTM in one application and open it in another. That doesn't work – try to open an Excel-created Web page from within Word, and Excel will start up to open it. What it does mean is that the same documents can be printed out, used directly on your desktop machine and made available to others via the Internet or your organisation's intranet *without any extra work*!

That brochure you produced in Word can be printed for use in the showroom or put on the Web for on-line customers. Your PowerPoint presentation will become a set of linked Web pages. These are good, but there's better! With Excel – and Access if you have it – you can publish interactive pages. Visitors will be able to enter their own information and have it processed and the results displayed from the page. Here's how to create an Excel page with added interactivity.

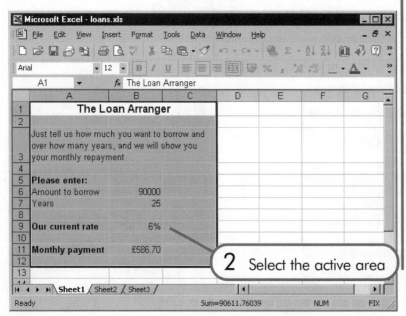

1 Create the sheet

2 Select the active area

1 Create the spread-sheet. In the Protection tab of the Format Cells dialog box, unlock the cells where visitors can enter data, then use Tools > Protection > Protect Sheet to lock the rest. Save the sheet as normal, as a backup.

2 Select the active area.

3 Open the File menu and select Save As Web Page…

4 Set the *Selection* as the Save option.

5 Tick Add interactivity.

6 Click Change Title... and enter a title to go on the page, if wanted.

7 Enter the Filename.

8 Click Publish... to send the page directly to your Web server.

Or

9 Click Save to save it to file for publishing later.

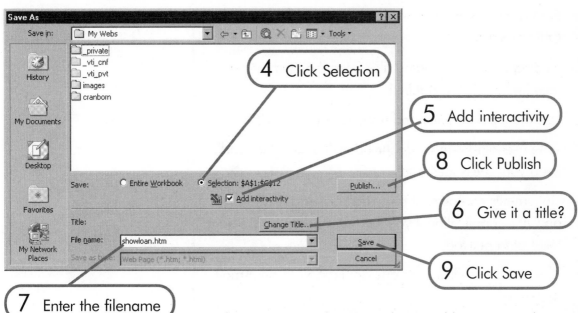

4 Click Selection

5 Add interactivity

8 Click Publish

6 Give it a title?

7 Enter the filename

9 Click Save

The page viewed in IE5 – the Monthly payment changes when new values are entered for the Amount or Years

Take note

Web pages created in other applications can be inserted into documents, just as objects or copied blocks can be. The main advantage of inserted Web pages is that they can have added interactivity.

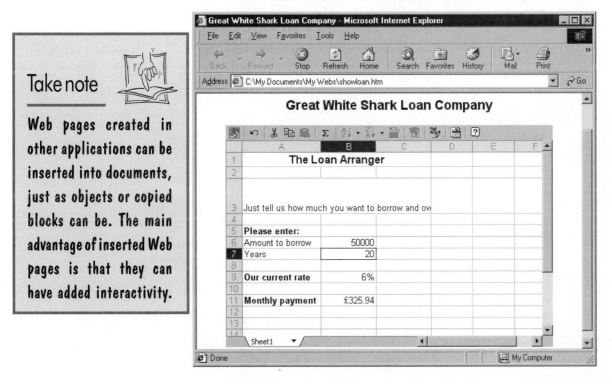

Summary

❑ Easy access to the Internet has been built into all the Office applications.

❑ Finding and downloading files from the Internet can take longer than you think!

❑ Use the Inbox to fetch and reply to your e-mail.

❑ When sending e-mail, do include a Subject line, and keep your messages brief.

❑ Documents can be sent by e-mail or fax directly from an Office application if you have a modem or are on a local area network.

❑ You can attach files from any application to an e-mail message.

❑ Hyperlinks can be used to link to files stored in public folders, or to Web pages and files on the Internet.

❑ Documents created in any Office application can be saved as Web pages. With Excel you can create inter-active pages.

11 Help!

Office Assistant

Office Assistant is a friendly front-end to the Help system. It keeps an eye on what you are doing, so that, when you call on it for Help, it will be ready with some likely topics. If it has guessed wrong – as it often does – you simply tell it what you need Help with, and it will come up with the goods.

Basic steps

1 If the Assistant is not visible, click the query icon to wake it up.

2 A relevant topic may be listed – if it is, click on it to display the page.

3 Type a word or phrase to describe the Help you want.

4 Click Search.

5 You will be offered a list of topics – click the one that is closest to your question.

❑ The Help window will open and display the page. For more on navigating Help, go on to page 186.

1 Wake the Assistant

Document1 - Microsoft Word

File Edit View Insert Format Tools Table Window Help

How do I get bullets

Normal + Right   Times New Roman   10   **B** *I* U

What would you like to do?

- Modify bulleted or numbered list formats
- Troubleshoot bulleted and numbered lists
- Convert bullets to numbers and vice versa
- Remove bullets or numbering
- Add bullets or numbering
- See more...

How do I get bullets

Options   Search

Office Assistant
Office Assistant is a friendly ...ps an eye on what you are
doing, so that, when you c... some likely topics. If it has
guessed wrong – as it often ...od help with, and it will
come up with the goods.

Page 1   Sec 1   1   At 4.1cm   Col 24   REC K EXT OVR English (U.K

5 Pick a topic

There may be more topics – click here to see them

3 Type a question

Typing 'bullets' alone would have been enough

4 Click Search

If you want the Assistant out of the way, right-click on it and select Hide from the short menu

Basic steps

❑ Setting the level

1 Click Options on the Assistant's dialog box or on its right-click menu.

2 Set the Options.

3 Clear the Use the Office Assistant checkbox if not wanted.

4 Click [OK].

❑ Asking for Help

5 Type a word or phrase into the Ask a Question box and press [Enter].

Levels of assistance

The Assistant has eight alternative 'personalities' for you to choose from, and – rather more usefully – a set of options to control how it works.

You can turn the Assistant off completely if you find it more irritating than entertaining (many people do)! You can still ask for Help, in exactly the same way, by typing your questions into the box at the top right of the application window.

Go to the Gallery to pick a new Assistant

2 Set options

3 Turn it off?

You can turn tips off when you no longer need them – see page 189 for more on tips.

4 Click OK

5 Enter a question

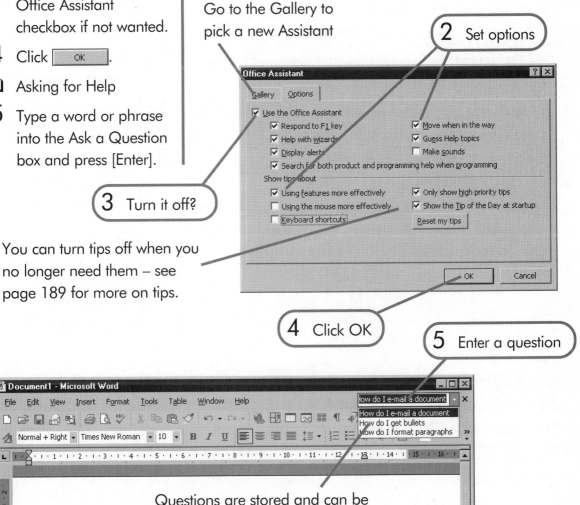

Questions are stored and can be recalled from the drop-down list

183

The Help system

If you use the Office Assistant to access the Help system, all you normally see is a page of Help, but there is more to it than this. Click the Show button, on the left of the toolbar, and a new panel opens. Its tabs gives you three ways to find Help.

Contents tab

This approach treats the Help pages as a book. Scan through the headings to find a section that seems to cover what you want, and open that to see the page titles. (Some sections have sub-sections, making it a 2 or 3-stage process to get to page titles.)

At first, the Help page will only show an overview of the topic. More detailed Help can be had in two ways:

- Within the text, some words are in blue, and become underlined when you point to them. Click on these to open up an explanation of the term.

- Subheadings, with arrows to their left – also in blue and becoming underlined when under the cursor – can be opened up. These typically give step by step instructions for performing tasks.

Basic steps

1 Click ⬚ the Show button.

2 Click the Contents tab if this panel is not at the front already.

3 Click ⊞ open a book – or ⊟ to close one.

4 Click ⬚ or the page title to see a page.

5 Click on word in blue to see an explanation.

6 Click on a subheading to to display its text.

7 Use the ⬅ and ➡ buttons to move be-tween visited pages.

8 When you have found the Help you want, click on the application window to hide Help or click x| to close Help.

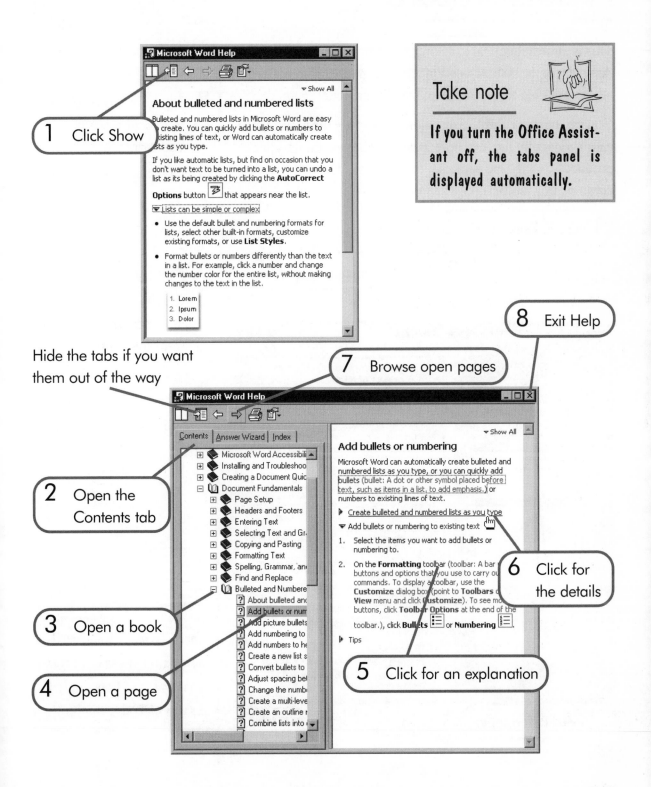

1 Click Show

Take note

If you turn the Office Assistant off, the tabs panel is displayed automatically.

About bulleted and numbered lists

Bulleted and numbered lists in Microsoft Word are easy to create. You can quickly add bullets or numbers to existing lines of text, or Word can automatically create lists as you type.

If you like automatic lists, but find on occasion that you don't want text to be turned into a list, you can undo a list as its being created by clicking the **AutoCorrect**

Options button 🐬 that appears near the list.

▼ Lists can be simple or complex

- Use the default bullet and numbering formats for lists, select other built-in formats, customize existing formats, or use **List Styles**.

- Format bullets or numbers differently than the text in a list. For example, click a number and change the number color for the entire list, without making changes to the text in the list.

  1. Lorem
  2. Ipsum
  3. Dolor

8 Exit Help

Hide the tabs if you want them out of the way

7 Browse open pages

Microsoft Word Help

Contents | Answer Wizard | Index

- Microsoft Word Accessibili
- Installing and Troubleshoo
- Creating a Document Quic
- Document Fundamentals
  - Page Setup
  - Headers and Footers
  - Entering Text
  - Selecting Text and Gr.
  - Copying and Pasting
  - Formatting Text
  - Spelling, Grammar, an
  - Find and Replace
  - Bulleted and Numbere
    - About bulleted and
    - Add bullets or num
    - Add picture bullets
    - Add numbering to
    - Add numbers to he
    - Create a new list s
    - Convert bullets to
    - Adjust spacing bet
    - Change the numbe
    - Create a multi-leve
    - Create an outline r
    - Combine lists into

2 Open the Contents tab

3 Open a book

4 Open a page

Add bullets or numbering

Microsoft Word can automatically create bulleted and numbered lists as you type, or you can quickly add bullets (bullet: A dot or other symbol placed before text, such as items in a list, to add emphasis.) or numbers to existing lines of text.

▶ Create bulleted and numbered lists as you type

▼ Add bullets or numbering to existing text

1. Select the items you want to add bullets or numbering to.

2. On the **Formatting** toolbar (toolbar: A bar buttons and options that you use to carry ou commands. To display a toolbar, use the **Customize** dialog box (point to **Toolbars** o **View** menu and click **Customize**). To see mo buttons, click **Toolbar Options** at the end of the toolbar.), click **Bullets** 📋 or **Numbering** 📋.

▶ Tips

6 Click for the details

5 Click for an explanation

185

Answer Wizard

This is almost identical to asking a question through the Office Assistant or the **Ask a question** box. The main difference is that all the possible topics are displayed in the panel.

You can type in complete questions, or simply the most significant words. In the example below 'table columns change' produces exactly the same set of topics as 'How do I change columns in a table?'

Basic steps

1 Switch to the Answer Wizard tab.

2 Type a word or phrase to describe the Help you want.

3 Click Search.

4 You will be offered a list of topics – click the one that is closest to your question.

5 Click on the subheadings that interest you to read their text.

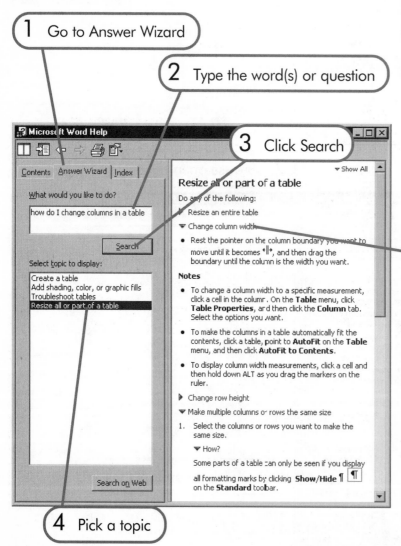

1 Go to Answer Wizard

2 Type the word(s) or question

3 Click Search

4 Pick a topic

5 Click to read the subtopic

Tip

There is more Help available online if you can't find what you need here – click Search on Web to go for it.

186

Using the Index

Basic steps

1 Click the Index tab.

2 Start to type a word in the keyword box, then select it from the list.

3 Click Search .

4 Enter a second word and search again.

5 Select a topic.

The Answer Wizard will locate the main Help pages on any topic, but if you want to dig deeper, try the Index. Searching for a word here will track down every page on which it occurs – and the Help system is very thoroughly indexed! The best way to use it is to give two or more words, to focus onto the most relevant pages.

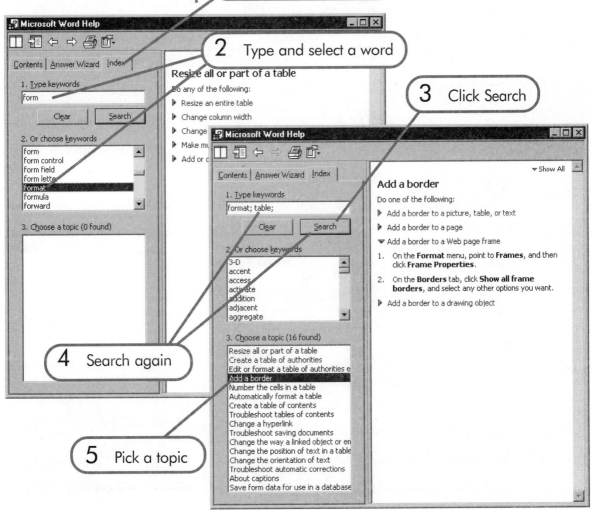

1 Open the Index tab

2 Type and select a word

3 Click Search

4 Search again

5 Pick a topic

Resize all or part of a table

Do any of the following:

▶ Resize an entire table

▶ Change column width

▶ Change

▶ Make m

▶ Add or c

Add a border

Do one of the following:

▶ Add a border to a picture, table, or text

▶ Add a border to a page

▼ Add a border to a Web page frame

1. On the **Format** menu, point to **Frames**, and then click **Frame Properties**.

2. On the **Borders** tab, click **Show all frame borders**, and select any other options you want.

▶ Add a border to a drawing object

187

What's This?

Office's icons, menus and dialog boxes are designed to be intuitive – which is great, as long as you know how to intuit! However, when you first start to use these applications, you may need a little prompting. *What's This?* will tell you about the buttons and menu items in the main application window.

Once you open a dialog box or menu, you can no longer get to the What's This? command, but the Help is still at hand. Most dialog boxes have a query icon ? at the top right, which does the same job, and – no matter what you are doing – pressing **[Shift]** and **[F1]** will usually start the What's This? Help.

Basic steps

- ☐ In the main window
- **1** Open the Help menu and select What's This?
- ☐ On a dialog box
- **2** Click ? or ↖.
- ☐ On a menu (or anywhere)
- **3** Press [Shift] + [F1].
- **4** Click the ↖? cursor on the item that you want to know about.
- **5** After you have read the Help box, click anywhere to close it.

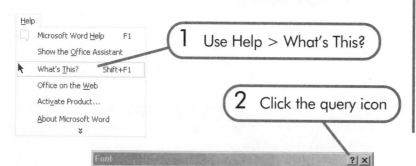

1 Use Help > What's This?

2 Click the query icon

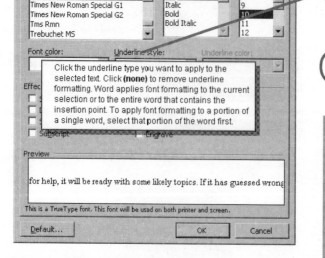

Click the underline type you want to apply to the selected text. Click **(none)** to remove underline formatting. Word applies font formatting to the current selection or to the entire word that contains the insertion point. To apply font formatting to a portion of a single word, select that portion of the word first.

4 Point and click for Help

5 Click anywhere to close

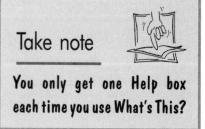

Take note

You only get one Help box each time you use What's This?

Basic steps

Tips and ScreenTips

☐ When the light is on

1 Click on the Office Assistant or the light icon to get the tip.

2 Select the new – or an earlier – tip.

3 If the tips don't help, ask a question and search as normal.

If ever you see   on Office Assistant, it has a tip related to your last action or to the last error report. The tips that crop up during a session are stored in the bubble, and can be read at any time

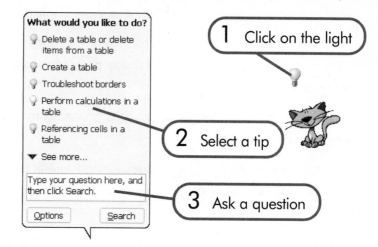

1 Click on the light

2 Select a tip

3 Ask a question

Tip

The startup Tip of the Day, and 'low priority' tips can be turned off through the Assistant's Options – see page 183.

ScreenTips

These are little prompts that appear when you pause the mouse over a tool button, to tell you its name and its shortcut keys. The tips can be turned on or off through the **Options** tab of the **Toolbars > Customize** dialog box.

Use Tools > Customize to open this dialog box

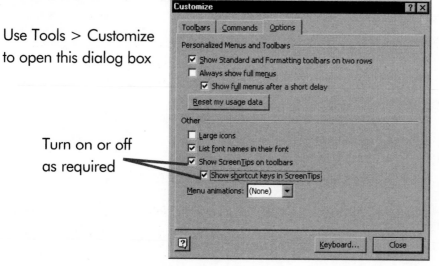

Turn on or off as required

If you mainly work through the keyboard, not the mouse, the shortcuts save time

Summary

- ❏ Help is always available.

- ❏ Office Assistant is a friendly front-end to the Help system. It will offer appropriate Help when needed, and can handle questions written in simple English.

- ❏ Office Assistant has several personalities – choose the one that suits you – or turn it off if you prefer to work without it.

- ❏ Use the Contents panel when you are browsing to see what topics are covered.

- ❏ You can get Help by asking a question in the Ask a question box of the application window or in the Answer Wizard tab of Help.

- ❏ Use the Index to go directly to the Help on a specified operation or object.

- ❏ For help in a dialog box or panel, use What's this? or click the query icon and point to the item.

- ❏ If you hold the cursor over an icon, a brief prompt will pop up to tell you what it does.

- ❏ The Tip of the Day at start up can be switched off if no longer wanted. Tips are stored and can be reviewed at any time.

Index